The Complete Book of Speed and Agility Football Drills

Jerry Tolley

COACHES CHOICE™

ISBN: 978-1-58518-085-1
Library of Congress Control Number: 2007943230
Cover design: Roger W. Rybkowski
Book layout: Roger W. Rybkowski
Front cover photo: Contra Costa Times/Mark DuFrene/ZUMA Press

Coaches Choice
P.O. Box 1828
Monterey, CA 93942
www.coacheschoice.com

Dedication

Dal Shealy

The desire to recognize and honor Dal Shealy, for his long and devoted commitment to the game of football and especially for his leadership of the Fellowship of Christian Athletes, was the motivating force behind the development of this book.

Dal Shealy, a native of Batesburg, South Carolina, is a product of Batesburg-Leesville High School. As a popular student-athlete, he gained all-State football honors and served as president of his junior and senior classes.

Dal attended Carson-Newman College, where he was a four-year starter and gained all-Tennessee and honorable mention all-American honors. At his Alma Mater, he was named to the all-century football team, inducted in the school's hall of fame, received the Carson-Newman Distinguished Alumni Award, and has served on the college's Board of Trustees. He also served his country as a lieutenant in the United States Marines.

Coach Shealy was a highly successful football coach. During his 27 years on the gridiron, he headed programs at Mars Hill College, Carson-Newman College, and the University of Richmond. He served as assistant head coach or offensive coordinator at Baylor, Tennessee, Auburn, and Iowa State. As head coach at Carson-Newman, he led the Eagles to the national title game in 1972. At Richmond, he led the Spiders to the NCAA I-AA playoffs in 1984 and 1987.

In reinstating football programs at Mars Hill, Carson-Newman, and Richmond, Dal received a number of coaching honors, including conference, district, state, regional, and national coach-of-the-year awards. In 1997, he received the All-American Football Foundation Johnny Vaught Lifetime Achievement Award. In 2002, he also received the

Outstanding Contribution to Amateur Football Award from the National Football Foundation and College Hall of Fame.

Dal is an author, inventor, and a nationally renowned speaker at clinics, banquets, seminars, assemblies, churches, and conventions. He has written two books, including, *One Way 2 Play!: Drug Free and One Way 2 Play!: Game Plan for Coaches.*

A devout Christian, Dal was first introduced to the Fellowship of Christian Athletes in the mid-1960s and served as a huddle coach at each school at which he coached. In January 1989, he began his professional association with the FCA as the executive vice president, and in 1992, he was named president. Under his superb leadership, the FCA transformed itself through what was called the Team FCA initiative with Jesus Christ and the Bible gaining the prominent middle position between Team and FCA. During the 40-month initiative, a vision statement was conceived, and the focus of the FCA was narrowed to encompass four core values: integrity, teamwork, serving and excellence. These values, along with the FCA's four Cs (coaches, campus, camps, and community), formed the backdrop for the restructuring effort.

When Dal took over the presidency, the organization was under the burden of a heavy debt, but as the 40-month program gained fruition, the FCA became debt-free and was housed in a greatly expanded complex with a comprehensive training center. In March 2005, Dal retired from his presidency and took his current position as the executive director of the Fellowship of Christian Athletes Football Coaches' Ministry.

At his side throughout his professional career was his wife, Barbara, who contributed to the FCA's success by being a beacon of light for coaches' wives as well as initiating the *Behind The Bench* quarterly newsletter, which gained a circulation of over 8700. Dal and Barbara have three children and 11 grandchildren. Together, they are spiritual role models for all of us.

Grant Teaff
Executive Director
American Football Coaches Association

Fisher DeBerry
Former Football Coach
The United States Air Force Academy

Acknowledgments

My sincere appreciation is expressed to Coach Bobby Bowden, head football coach at Florida State University, and Fisher DeBerry, the retired head football coach at the United States Air Force Academy, for serving as honorary co-chairs for this special effort to honor Dal Shealy. Gratitude is also expressed to Mel Tjeerdsma, head football coach at Northwest Missouri State University and the 2006 president of the American Football Coaches Association, for his guidance and assistance.

Thanks also to the many coaches who submitted football drills to make this book possible. Their commitments to honor Dal Shealy and to promote the time-honored tradition of the sharing of ideas among the coaching fraternity made the editorship of this book both an honor and a joy.

Gratitude is expressed to Kim Werr for her administrative support and her masterful job of typing the text, as well as to Maggie Byerly for her editorial assistance. Their valuable contributions helped make this publication a reality.

A loving appreciation is given to my wonderful wife, Joanie, for her patience, understanding, and support.

Foreword

On behalf of our Florida State University football program, I enthusiastically introduce Jerry Tolley's *The Complete Book of Speed and Agility Football Drills* to the coaching community.

Along with many other football coaches, I believe that football drills that help to develop and maintain speed and agility are the hallmark of every successful football program. Coaches are always looking for that one very special speed and agility drill that will give their team the winning edge on game day. Jerry's comprehensive book of speed and agility drills will do just that.

This drill book contains speed and agility drills for every position fundamental to football. Each drill is presented with the specific objective in mind, the equipment needed, essential coaching points, important safety considerations, and a detailed illustration.

Over 100 of the most successful collegiate and professional coaches from across the country are featured in the book. Included are such nationally acclaimed coaches as: Frank Beamer, Mack Brown, John Fox, Paul Johnson, Greg Schiano, Jim Tressel, and Tommy Tuberville. As you can see, it is truly a book of legendary proportions.

Bobby Bowden
Head Football Coach
Florida State University

Contents

1

Running Back Drills

Wave Drill

Paul Johnson
Head Coach, United States Naval Academy

Objective: To develop agility and speed. Incorporated are skills related to ball security.

Equipment Needed: Six large half-moon agility bags, two cones, and a football

Description:

- Lay six half-moon agility bags one yard apart and perpendicular to a selected yard line. A cone is placed seven yards beyond each end of the bag area.
- Position a row of running backs adjacent to the drill area.
- The coach stands in front of the row of bags, and a player (manager) is positioned on the opposite side (see the diagram).
- On the coach's command, the first running back, carrying a football, assumes the football ready position at the center of the bags.
- On the coach's second command, blowing the whistle and giving a hand signal, the running back moves laterally over the bags in the direction the coach has signaled.
- The coach alternates his directional commands until the running backs have changed directions three or four times.
- Each time the running back changes directions, the player (manager) standing on the backside of the row of bags tries to strike the football from behind in an ascending blow in an attempt to cause a fumble.
- If the football is fumbled, the running back recovers the football, using the proper fumble-recovery technique.
- If the football is not fumbled (and after the final directional signal is given), the coach gives a burst call, and the player sprints over the remaining bags and past the cone on that side.
- The drill continues until all running backs have had a sufficient number of repetitions.

Coaching Points:

- Always check to see that the running backs are in the correct football ready position before starting the drill.
- Insist that the drill be conducted at full speed.
- The directional changes should be done in short bursts with only three or four changes in direction.

- Instruct the running backs to always maintain eye contact with the coach and to never look down.
- Emphasize the importance of carrying the football properly and maintaining ball security at all times.
- In finishing the drill, insist that the running back sprints past the cone on the side of the last directional signal.
- If the football is fumbled and recovered, the coach should give immediate feedback on ball security and review the proper techniques of fumble recovery.

Safety Considerations:

- Proper warm-up should precede the drill.
- Full equipment should be worn.
- The drill area should be clear of all foreign articles.

Variations:

- Vary the number of bags.
- The drill can be used with all ballcarrying positions.

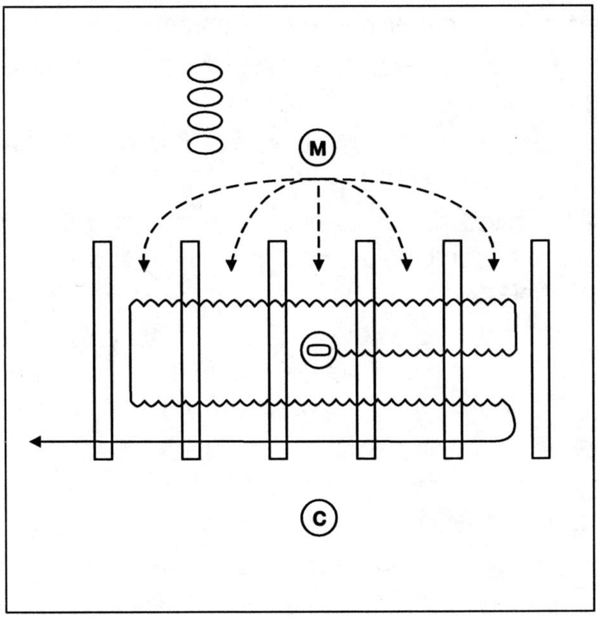

Blaster Circuit Drill

Paul Hamilton
Head Coach, Brevard College

Objective: To develop agility and speed. Incorporated are skills related to receiving a handoff or pitch, running with and securing the football, and reacting to a potential tackler.

Equipment Needed: A blaster, cones, and footballs

Description:

- Align a row of running backs seven yards behind and parallel to a blaster.
- A coach is positioned two yards in front of the blaster in a handoff relationship with the row of running backs.
- Other running backs are aligned on the backside of the blaster in two rows facing each other, forming a gauntlet (see the diagram).
- A cone is placed five yards beyond the gauntlet area.
- Six additional cones are placed seven yards outside of the blaster and on each side of the drill area. On one side, the cones are placed in a straight row, and on the other side, they are placed in a staggered alignment (see the diagram).
- A running back (manager) is positioned five yards behind the end of each row of cones, as noted in the preceding description.
- On the coach's cadence and snap count, the first running back drives from his stance and receives the handoff from the coach.
- After receiving the handoff, the running back explodes through the blaster and secures the football through the gauntlet area as the players try to strip the football from the running back.
- As the running back approaches the cone placed five yards past the gauntlet area, he cuts either left or right and sprints to the cones that are placed on either side of the blaster.
- Depending on which way the running back cuts, he either sprints down the sideline on the outside of the cones on the side of the blaster, or he runs in and out of the cones placed on the other side of the blaster.
- When the running back runs past these cones, he reacts to and cuts off the forward movement of the running back (manager) who is positioned five yards past the cone area.
- The drill continues until all running backs have had a sufficient number of repetitions moving through the drill.

Coaching Points:

- Always check to see that all running backs are aligned correctly and are in their proper stances before starting the drill.
- Insist that the drill be conducted at full speed.
- Instruct the running backs to keep their shoulders low and squared as they explode through the blaster, and to secure the football as they run through the gauntlet area.
- Emphasize the importance of making a sharp cut at the cone beyond the gauntlet area and maintaining a good body lean and balance while sprinting through or past the cones on either side of the blaster.
- Insist that the running backs sprint 10 yards upfield after they cut off the step of the manager who is positioned at the end of the drill.

Safety Considerations:

- Proper warm-up should precede the drill.
- The drill area should be clear of all foreign articles.
- It is imperative that shoulder pads and helmets be worn with chinstraps snapped.
- Instruct the players in the gauntlet area not to be abusive as they strive to strip the football from the running backs.

Variations:

- In initiating the drill, the coach can either hand off, pitch, or throw the football to the running backs.
- The drill can be used with all ballcarrying positions.

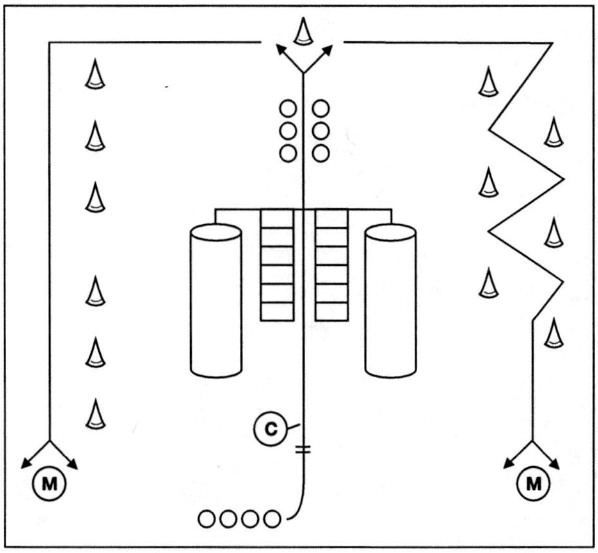

Accelerator Drill

Tommy Bowden
Head Coach, Clemson University

Objective: To develop agility and speed. Incorporated are skills related to catching the football.

Equipment Needed: Six cones and footballs

Description:

- Place five cones on a selected yard line that represents the proper alignment of a center, the offensive guards, and offensive tackles.
- A sixth cone is placed 15 yards downfield beyond the guard and tackle positions (see the diagram).
- A quarterback (coach), holding a football, is aligned in the designated shotgun position.
- Position a running back in the designated offset shotgun alignment (see the diagram).
- Other running backs stand adjacent to the drill area.
- On the coach's cadence and snap count, the running back executes a five-yard stop pass route in front of the offensive guard and tackle positions.
- The running back snaps his head around, focuses his eyes on the coach, and catches the thrown football.
- After receiving the pass, the running back makes an inside head fake against an imaginary defender, and then pivots to the outside and accelerates 10 yards upfield past the cone.
- The drill continues until all running backs have had a sufficient number of repetitions from both a left and right shotgun alignment.

Coaching Points:

- Always check to see that the running backs are aligned correctly and are in their proper stances before starting the drill.
- Insist that the drill be conducted at full speed.
- Emphasize the importance of executing the five-yard pass route correctly, with eyes focused on the coach and catching the football with the hands.

- Insist that after catching and securing the football, the running back properly executes an inside head fake and outside pivot against the imaginary defender (by doing so, the running back will create space between himself and the defender).
- Emphasize the importance of accelerating and sprinting full speed past the cone placed 10 yards upfield.

Safety Considerations:

- Proper warm-up should precede the drill.
- The drill area should be clear of all foreign articles.
- Instruct the returning pass-receiving running backs to stay well clear of the drill start area.

Variations:

- Substitute the imaginary defender with a real defender.
- The drill can be used with all ballcarrying positions.
- Have the pass-receiving running back accelerate various distances upfield (5 to 15 yards).

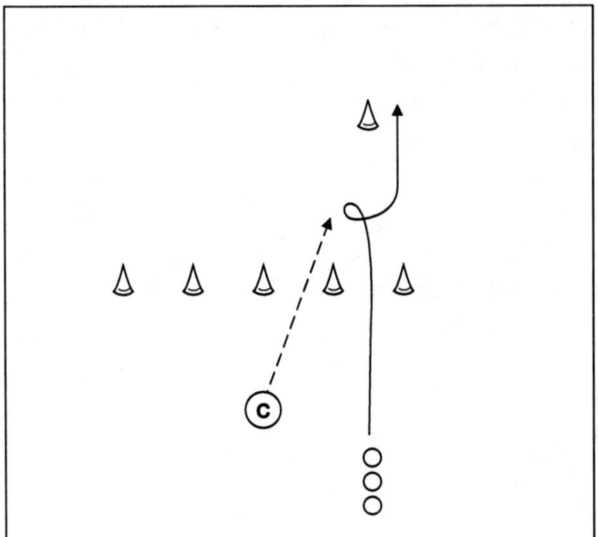

Staircase Drill

Kevin Higgins
Head Coach, The Citadel

Objective: To develop agility and speed. Incorporated are skills related to catching and carrying the football.

Equipment Needed: Six agility bags and footballs

Description:

- Place six agility bags in a staircase alignment (long end to short end), as shown in the diagram.
- Position a row of running backs adjacent to and in a front-facing alignment to the first bag.
- The coach, holding a football, is positioned five yards beyond and at the opposite end of the staircase of bags.
- On the coach's command, the first running back sprints over the first bag, moves laterally over the second bag, sprints over the third bag, and continues this pattern until all bags have been moved over.
- After moving laterally over the final bag, the coach flips the ball to the running back, who turns and sprints 10 yards upfield.
- When all running backs have completed the drill from the front-facing starting alignment to the first bag, the alignment is changed to a sideways alignment to the first agility bag.
- Again, on the coach's command, the first running back moves laterally over the first bag, sprints over the second bag, moves laterally over the third bag, and continues this pattern until all bags have been moved over.
- The drill continues until all running backs have had a sufficient number of repetitions in both a front-facing and sideways-facing alignment to the first bag.

Coaching Points:

- Always check to see that the running backs are in the football ready position before starting the drill.
- Insist that the drill be conducted at full speed.
- Emphasize the importance of always keeping the head up and the eyes focused forward.
- Instruct the running backs as they move over the bags to place each foot down as quickly as possible with a quick "one-two" foot placement before moving over the next bag.

- Instruct the running backs to keep a high knee action with their arms pumping as they move over and through the bags.
- In completing the drill, insist that the running backs sprint 10 yards upfield after they catch the flipped football from the coach.

Safety Considerations:

- Proper warm-up should precede the drill.
- The drill area should be clear of all foreign articles.

Variations:

- The drill can be used as a general speed and agility drill.
- The drill can be used with running backs carrying a football as they move over and through the bags.
- The coach can stand at various alignments adjacent to the bags and flip a football to the running backs as they move over and through the bags.

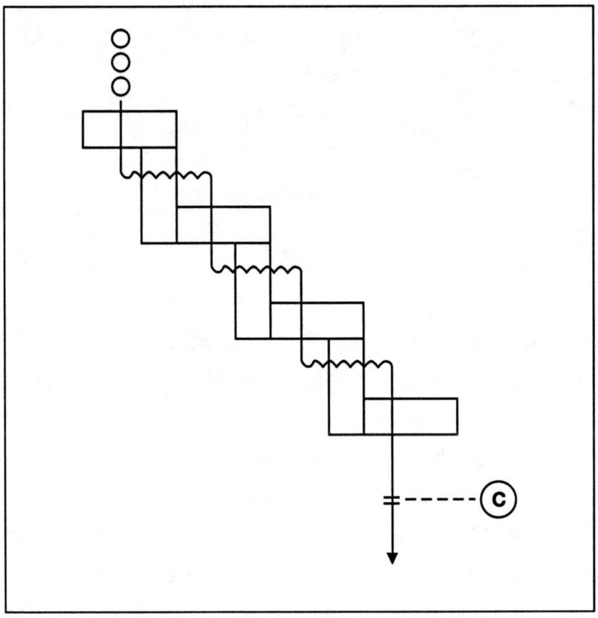

Box Drill

Ken Sparks
Head Coach, Carson-Newman College

Objective: To develop general agility and speed. Incorporated are skills related to avoiding contact.

Equipment Needed: None

Description:

- Mark off a five-yard square area.
- Align a running back (release back) on one side of the square and a blocking back on the other side of the square (see the diagram).
- Other release backs and blocking backs stand adjacent to the drill area.
- The coach is positioned behind the release back and to the left or right of the five-yard square.
- On the coach's command, the release back strives to avoid contact and cross the line being protected by the blocking back, who strives to engage the release back, driving him out of the five-yard square area.
- The drill is completed when the release back crosses the back line or when the coach blows his whistle.
- The drill continues until all running backs have had a sufficient number of repetitions.

Coaching Points:

- Remind participants that the drill is not a tackling drill. The release back's goal is to cross the line being protected by the blocker, and the blocker's goal is to block the release back out of the drill area.
- Always check to see that the release backs and blocking backs are in the football ready position before starting the drill.
- Instruct the release backs to keep a low center of gravity, avoid contact and cross the backline as close to the center of the line as possible.
- Instruct the blocking backs to maintain a good football position, with feet always moving, in contacting the release back.

Safety Considerations:

- Proper warm-up should precede the drill.
- Full equipment should be worn.
- The coach should closely monitor the intensity of the drill.
- Instruct the release back to avoid contact with the blocking back and to never run to overpower him.
- Instruct the blocking backs that they should not ever tackle the release back but to always block him out of the drill area.

Variation:

- The drill can be conducted in a 10-by-10-yard square area.

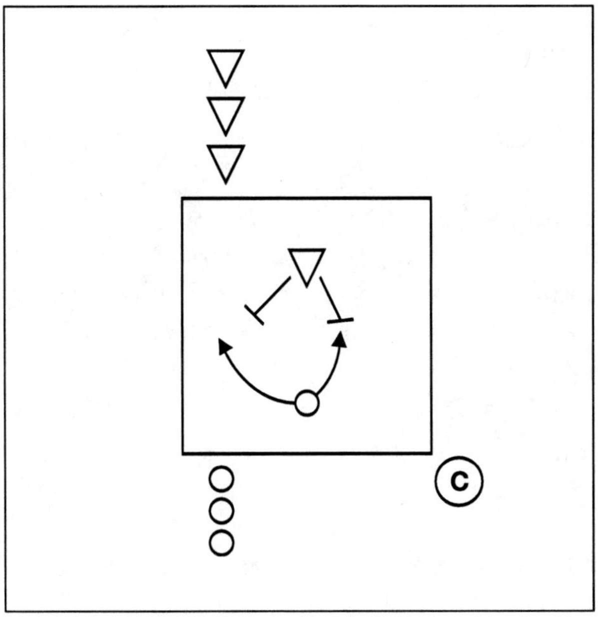

Breakout Drill

Jay Mills
Head Coach, Charleston Southern University

Objective: To develop general agility and speed. Incorporated are skills related to receiving a handoff and avoiding tacklers.

Equipment Needed: Footballs

Description:

- Position six defenders (one defensive lineman, two linebackers, and three defensive backs) in an inverted pyramid alignment, simulating the three levels of a defense (see the diagram).
- Position a running back in his stance and at the designated alignment to the first defender (a defensive lineman).
- Other running backs stand adjacent to the drill area.
- The coach (quarterback) is positioned at the mesh point for the handoff.
- On the coach's cadence and snap count, the first running back drives from his stance and receives the handoff from the coach.
- As the running back approaches the first-level defender (the lineman), the defender will lean either left or right. The running back will break away from the defender's move and proceed to the next level defender(s).
- This procedure is repeated at the second and third levels as the running back breaks away at each level.
- The drill ends with the running back sprinting past the third-level defender(s).

Coaching Points:

- Always check to see that the running backs are aligned correctly and are in their proper stances before starting the drill.
- Insist that the drill be conducted at full speed.
- Instruct the running backs to take the designated steps to the mesh point while maintaining the proper body lean.
- Emphasize the importance of keeping the eyes focused on the defender as the running back forms a pocket and secures the football as he proceeds through the mesh point.

- Instruct the running backs not to make their breakaway until the defender has leaned either left or right.
- Insist that the running backs carry the football correctly and use the proper techniques in changing the football from one arm to the other.

Safety Considerations:

- Proper warm-up should precede the drill.
- The drill area should be clear of all foreign articles.
- Instruct returning running backs to stay well clear of the drill area.

Variations:

- Use assorted backfield alignments and actions.
- Vary the depth and width alignments of the three levels of defenders.

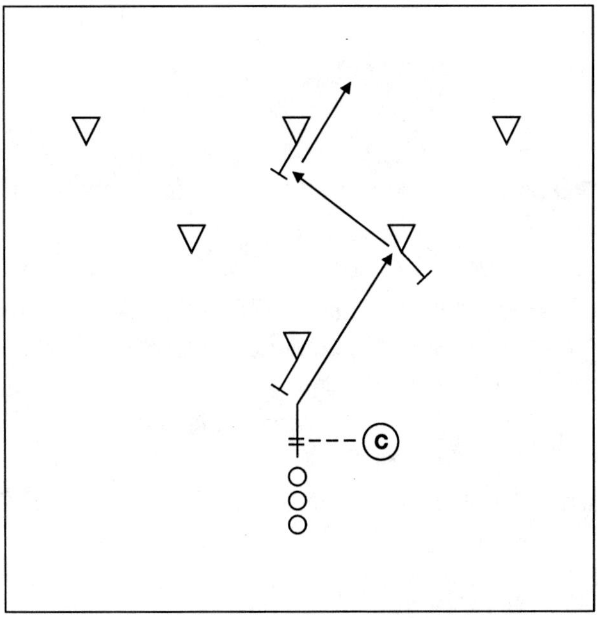

Accelerate-Decelerate Drill

Scott Browne
Assistant Coach, Elon University

Objective: To develop agility and speed. Incorporated are skills related to acceleration and deceleration.

Equipment Needed: Six cones and footballs

Description:

- Place two cones two yards apart on a selected yard line.
- Place four additional cones at a 45-degree staggered-angle alignment and the first three each being five yards apart and upfield from the set of paired cones. The fourth cone is also placed at a 45-degree angle and 10 yards upfield from the third cone (see the diagram).
- Position a running back, holding a football, between the two paired cones.
- Other running backs stand adjacent to the drill area.
- The coach is positioned to the right of the drill area.
- On the coach's cadence and snap count, the first running back drives from his stance with arms pumping and sprints past the first cone positioned five yards in front of the paired cones.
- When the running back passes the cone, he plants his outside foot and slides laterally to the second cone keeping his arm *pumping* and his shoulders squared.
- When the running back passes the second cone, he decelerates his slide and arm pumping while still keeping his shoulders squared.
- When he passes the third cone, he accelerates again, pumping the arms, and sprints 10 yards past the last cone.
- The drill continues until all drill participants have had a sufficient number of repetitions.

Coaching Points:

- Always check to see that the running backs are aligned correctly and in their proper stances before starting the drill
- Insist that the drill be conducted at full speed.
- Emphasize the importance of maintaining the proper arm-pumping speed in the appropriate areas of the drill.
- Instruct the running backs to always keep their eyes focused straight ahead.
- Insist that the running backs finish the drill by sprinting past the last cone.

Safety Considerations:

- Proper warm-up should precede the drill.
- The drill area should be clear of all foreign articles.
- Instruct the running backs to stay well clear of the drill-finish area.

Variations:

- Position hand shield holders along the slide paths to try to jam the football loose from the running backs.
- The drill can be used by all ballcarrying positions.

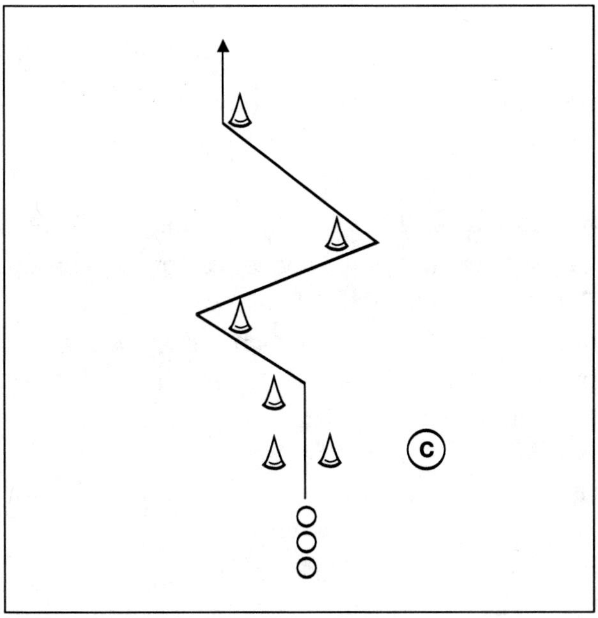

Cone Weave Drill

David Bennett
Head Coach, Coastal Carolina University

Objective: To develop agility and speed. Incorporated are skills related to the executing the backpedal.

Equipment Needed: Seven cones

Description:

- Align eight cones, four on each of two selected yard lines, in a staggered relationship to each other. Five yards should separate each row of cones (see the diagram).
- Position a row of running backs adjacent to one of the end cones.
- The coach is positioned in the middle of the drill area.
- On coach's command, the first running back drives from his stance and sprints past the first cone on the front-facing yard line.
- The running back backpedals back past the third cone on the original yard line.
- The running back continues this sequence of sprinting forward and then backpedaling until all cones have been passed.
- The drill continues until all running backs have had a sufficient number of repetitions, moving from both the left and right sides of the cones.

Coaching Points:

- Always check to see that the running backs are in their proper stances before starting the drill.
- Insist that the drill be conducted at full speed.
- In the sprint components of the drill, insist that the running backs keep their hips low, accelerate hard with their arms pumping and eyes focused straight ahead.
- Instruct the running backs to maintain a low center of gravity, with the weight forward as they execute the backpedal.

Safety Considerations:

- Proper warm-up should precede the drill.
- The drill area should be clear of all foreign articles.

Variation:

- The drill can be used for all positions.

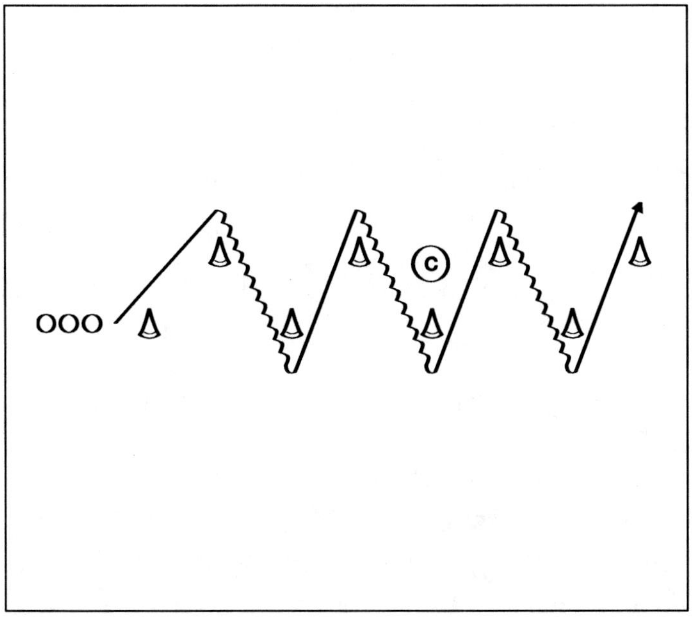
OOO
C

Cut Drill

Dale Steele
Head Coach, Campbell University

Objective: To develop agility and speed. Incorporates skills related to making sharp and quick cuts in order to avoid a tackler.

Equipment Needed: Two cones, five half-moon agility bags, and footballs

Description:

- Lay five half-moon agility bags three yards apart and perpendicular to a yard line (see the diagram).
- Place a cone five yards from each end of the row of bags.
- Align a row of running backs adjacent to the cone at either end of the row of bags.
- The coach is positioned adjacent to the mid-point of the drill area.
- On the coach's command, the first running back, carrying a football, sprints to the corner of the first bag, plants his right foot, and sprints to the corner of the second bag.
- At the corner of the second bag, the running back plants his left foot and sprints back to the corner of the third bag.
- The running back continues this sequence of sprinting to the corner of the next bag and planting the appropriate foot until all the bags have been passed.
- After all the bags have been passed, the running back sprints past the cone at the end of the drill area.
- The drill continues until all running backs have had a sufficient number of repetitions, moving both from the left and right through the bags.

Coaching Points:

- Always check to see that the running backs are in the proper football ready position before starting the drill.
- Insist that the drill be conducted at full speed.
- Emphasize the importance of proper weight distribution and that footwork should be quick and precise.
- Instruct running backs to accelerate out of all cuts.
- Make sure the running backs are securing the football correctly (high and tight).
- Insist that the running backs finish the drill by sprinting past the cone at the end of the bags.

Safety Considerations:

- Proper warm-up should precede the drill.
- The drill area should be clear of all foreign articles.

Variations:

- Vary the distances between the bags.
- The drill can be used for all ballcarrying positions.

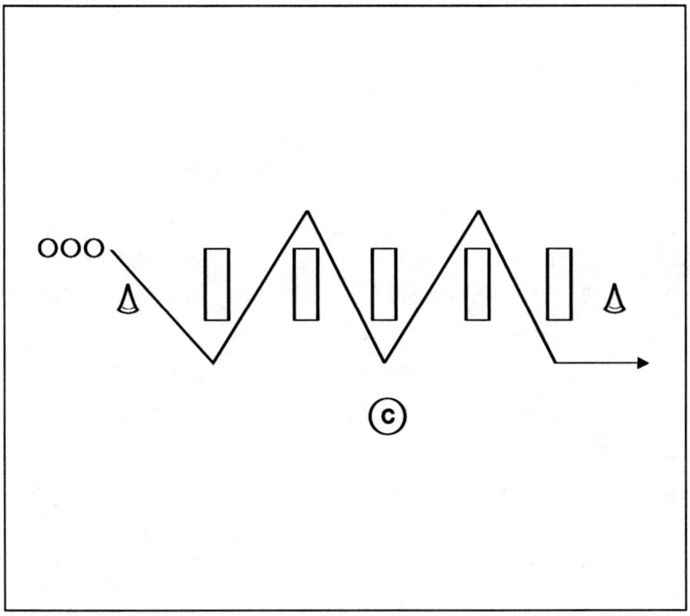

Four-Cone Cut Drill

Turner Gill
Assistant Coach, Green Bay Packers

Objective: To develop agility and speed. Incorporated are skills related to planting and driving off the back foot when making cuts and maintaining proper body alignment when running with the football.

Equipment Needed: Four cones, two dots, and a football

Description:

- Place two dots 15 yards apart and place four cones at three-yard depth intervals and in a staggered relationship between the dots. The width between the staggered cones is five yards (see the diagram).
- Align a row of running backs next to one of the dots.
- The coach is positioned next to the corresponding dots.
- On the coach's command, the first running back, carrying a football, sprints to the first cone, makes a hard plant with the right foot, and then sprints to the second cone.
- At the second cone, the running back makes a hard plant with the left foot.
- This sequence of sprinting to the next cone and hard planting with the appropriate foot continues until sprinting past the far dot.
- At the far dot, the running back places his left hand in the middle of the dot and completes a full 360-degree turn around the dot. After the 360-degree turn is completed, the running back repeats the sprinting and cutting sequence as he returns to the starting point (dot) of the drill.
- The drill continues until all running backs have had two repetitions, carrying the football under each arm.

Coaching Points:

- Always check to see that the running backs are in their proper stances before starting the drill.
- Insist that the drill be conducted at full speed.
- Make sure that the running backs execute the hard plant when making the cut at each cone.
- Instruct the running backs to always focus the eyes straight ahead and not to look down at the ground.

- Emphasize the importance of accelerating after each hard plant and cut and sprinting between cones.
- Insist that the running backs sprint past the dot after the hard foot plant at the last cone.

Safety Considerations:

- Proper warm-up should precede the drill.
- Alert running backs who are waiting to perform the drill to stay clear of the drill

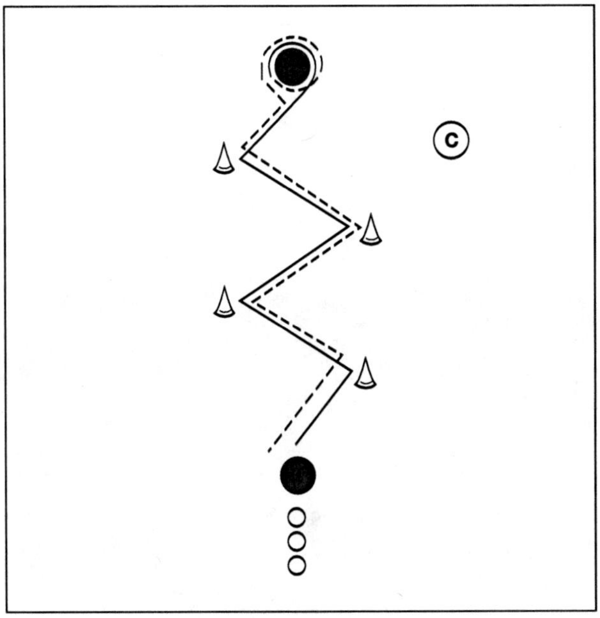

2

Quarterback Drills

Pocket Awareness Drill

Mack Brown
Head Coach, University of Texas

Objective: To develop agility and speed. Incorporated are skills related to gaining the feel of the passing pocket.

Equipment Needed: Four half-moon agility bags and football

Description:

- Align four half-moon agility bags one yard apart and perpendicular to a sideline (see the diagram).
- Position a row of quarterbacks just behind and to the right of the first bag.
- The coach stands 15 yards in front of and at the midpoint of the row of bags.
- On the coach's command, the first quarterback, holding the football in the pass ready position, slides up, around and back through the bags keeping his eyes on the coach at all times.
- After moving through the final bag and on the coach's second command ("Ball"), the quarterback passes the football to the coach.
- The drill continues until all quarterbacks have had a sufficient number of repetitions sliding up, around, and back in both directions through the bags.

Coaching Points:

- Always check to see that the quarterbacks are in the football ready position before starting the drill.
- Insist that the drill be conducted at full speed.
- Instruct the quarterbacks to always focus their eyes on the coach as they slide up, around, and back through the bags.
- Make sure the quarterback holds the football in the pass ready position throughout the drill.
- Make sure all quarterbacks practice the proper mechanics in throwing all passes.

Safety Considerations:

- Proper warm-up should precede the drill.
- The drill area (including the sideline area) should be clear of all foreign articles.

Variation:

- The drill can be used with receivers positioned at various spots downfield to simulate pass route ending points for the quarterbacks to throw passes to.

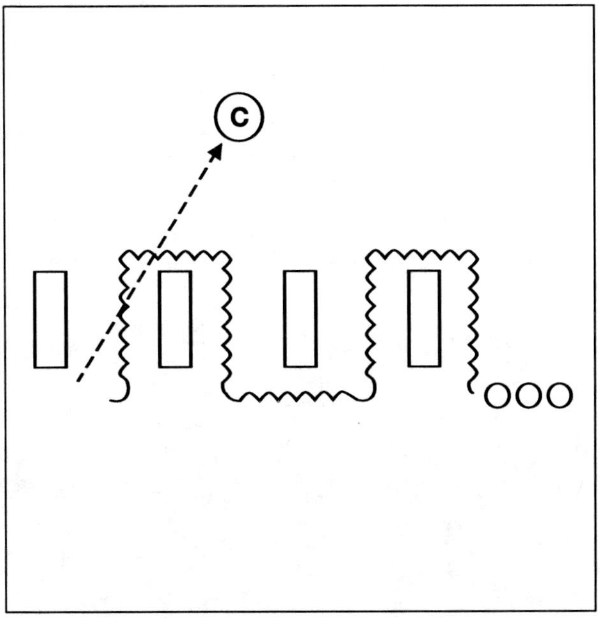

Pitch Drill

Jerry Tolley
Former Head Coach, Elon College (now Elon University)

Objective: To develop agility and speed. Incorporated are skills related to pitching a football on the option play.

Equipment Needed: Footballs

Description:

- Align two rows of quarterbacks five yards apart on two different yard lines and adjacent to a sideline. One of the quarterbacks in each row is holding a football (see the diagram).
- The coach is positioned adjacent to the drill area.
- On the coach's command, the first quarterback in each row runs across the football field, pitching the football back-and-forth.
- The drill continues until all quarterbacks have had a sufficient number of repetitions moving from both left and right across the field.

Coaching Points:

- Always check to see that all quarterbacks are in the proper football position before starting the drill.
- Insist that the drill be conducted at full speed.
- Instruct the quarterbacks as to the proper techniques in executing the pitch.
- Insist that the paired quarterbacks maintain a five-yard separation in crossing the field.

Safety Considerations:

- Proper warm-up should precede the drill.
- The drill area (including the sideline area) should be clear of all foreign articles.
- Alert quarterbacks who have finished the drill to stay well clear of the drill-finish area.

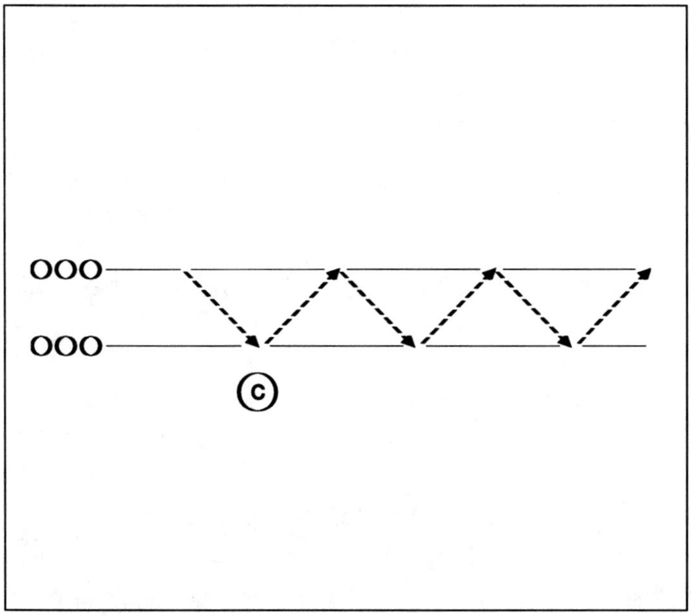
OOO
OOO
C

Pocket Footwork Wave Drill

Gregg Brandon
Head Coach, Bowling Green State University

Objective: To develop agility and speed. Incorporated are skills related to developing footwork, agility, and balance while moving in the passing pocket.

Equipment Needed: Three flat agility bags, a cone, and a football

Description:

- Align three flat agility bags one half yard apart and perpendicular to a selected yard line. Place a cone four yards in front of and to the outside of the first agility bag (see the diagram).
- Position a quarterback holding a football behind the cone.
- Other quarterbacks stand adjacent to the cone.
- The coach stands five yards in front of and at the midpoint of the bag area.
- On the coach's command, the first quarterback executes a five-step pass drop as the coach directs the quarterback with hand signals to slide right, left, up, back, and around the bags.
- On the coach's handclap, the quarterback will finish the drill by tucking the football away and sprinting past the coach.
- The drill continues until all quarterbacks have had a sufficient number of repetitions, starting from both the left and the right side of the bags.

Coaching Points:

- Always check to see that the quarterbacks are aligned correctly and in their proper stances with their shoulders parallel to the start line before beginning the drill.
- Insist that the drill be conducted at full speed.
- Instruct all quarterbacks to hold the football in the pass ready position throughout the drill.
- Instruct the quarterbacks as they slide left and right to kick slide with the back foot moving first, keeping their weight back and body balanced.
- Emphasize the importance of maintaining quick feet throughout the drill.
- Instruct the quarterbacks as they slide up and back through the bags to always lead with the direction leg first and then slide with the other leg, keeping their weight back and body balanced.
- Make sure all quarterbacks finish the drill by sprinting past the coach.

Safety Considerations:

- Proper warm-up should precede the drill.
- The drill area should be clear of all foreign articles.

Variations:

- Place a receiver in different spots downfield and have quarterbacks end the drill by throwing a pass.
- Increase the number of agility bags.

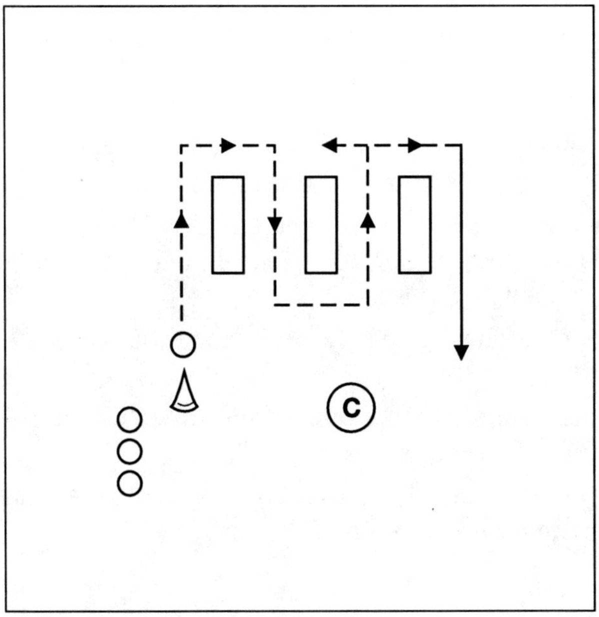

Zigzag Drill

Tommy Tuberville
Head Coach, Auburn University

Objective: To develop agility and speed. Incorporated are skills related to passing the football.

Equipment Needed: Eleven cones and a football

Description:

- Place 10 cones in a straight line and perpendicular to a selected yard line. One yard separates each cone. Another cone is placed 10 yards downfield from the last cone.
- Align a row of quarterbacks one yard behind and facing the first cone.
- Position a coach five yards from and at the midpoint of the cones.
- On the coach's command, the first quarterback, holding the football in the pass ready position, runs past the first cone, plants the outside foot, moves to the next cone, and again plants the outside foot.
- The run sequence continues until the quarterback has completed the run through the 10 cones.
- After passing the tenth cone, the quarterback tucks the football away and sprints past the cone placed 10 yards downfield.
- The drill continues until all quarterbacks have had a sufficient number of repetitions, starting from both ends of the drill.

Coaching Points:

- Always check to see that the quarterbacks are in their proper stances before starting the drill.
- Insist that the drill be conducted at full speed.
- Instruct the quarterback to always plant the outside foot in moving around each cone.
- Emphasize the importance of always holding the football at the pass ready position, with the head up and eyes focused forward.
- In finishing the drill, insist that all quarterbacks sprint past the downfield cone.

Safety Considerations:

- Proper warm-up should precede the drill.
- The drill area should be clear of all foreign articles.

Variations:

- Vary the distance between the cones.
- Stagger the cones.
- Place a receiver at the downfield cone and have quarterback throw a pass at some point along the 10-cone path.

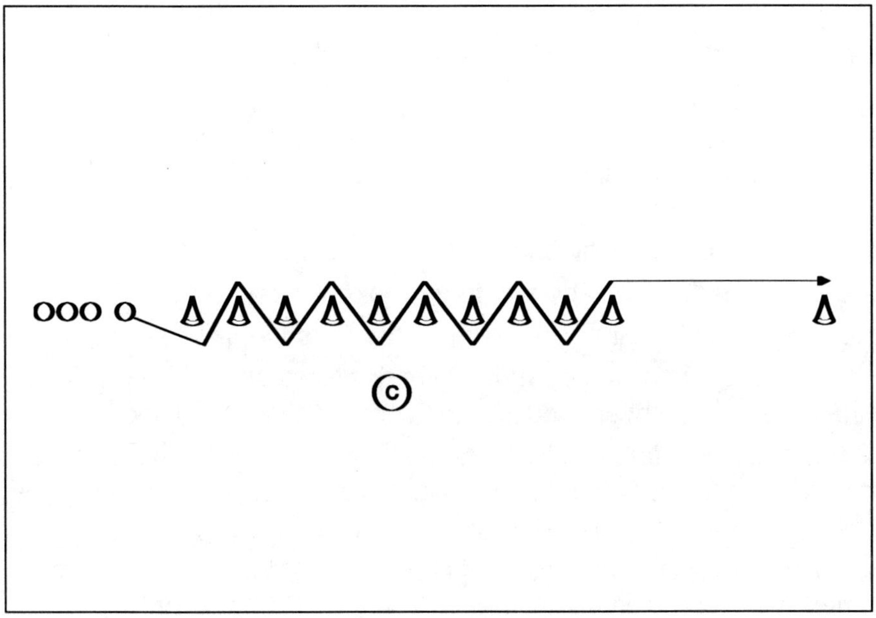

Three-Cone Change-of-Direction Drill

Jeff Jagodzinski
Head Coach, Boston College

Objective: To develop agility and speed. Incorporated are skills related to changing directions.

Equipment Needed: Eight cones

Description:

- Align three cones three to five yards apart on a selected yard line. A fourth cone designated as home is placed five yards behind the middle cone. Place four additional cones in a mirror alignment opposite the placement of the first four cones (see the diagram).
- Position a quarterback, lying on his stomach, behind each of the home cones.
- Other quarterbacks stand adjacent to each of the home cones.
- Position the coach to either the right or left side of the drill area.
- On the coach's command, each quarterback explodes off his stomach and sprints to the cone to his right and touches the cone with the right hand.
- The quarterbacks sprint back to the home cone, touching the home cone with the left hand. Quarterbacks sprint to the middle cone, touching it with the right hand, and then back to the home cone with a left-handed touch.
- The quarterbacks finish the drill by sprinting back to the left cone, touching it with the right hand, and then backpedaling straight back for five yards.
- Drill continues until all quarterbacks have had a sufficient number of repetitions, moving from both right to left and left to right from the home cone.

Coaching Points:

- Make sure all quarterbacks are lying on their stomachs before starting the drill.
- Insist that the drill be conducted at full speed.
- Instruct the quarterbacks to always touch the different cones with the designated hand.
- Insist that all quarterbacks turn and sprint with each change of direction (no shuffling).
- Emphasize the importance of keeping the hips down in reaching to touch each cone, and not bending over at the waist.

- The coach should try to match up quarterbacks with similar speed as each pair of quarterbacks takes their turn.
- Insist that all quarterbacks backpedal, at full speed, for five yards after touching the last cone.

Safety Considerations:

- Proper warm-up should precede the drill.
- The drill area should be clear of all foreign articles.
- Alert the quarterbacks who are waiting to perform the drill to stay clear of the drill-finish area.

Variations:

- The drill can be used by all positions.
- Vary the distance between the cones.
- Vary the starting positions (on the back, in the football ready position, etc.).

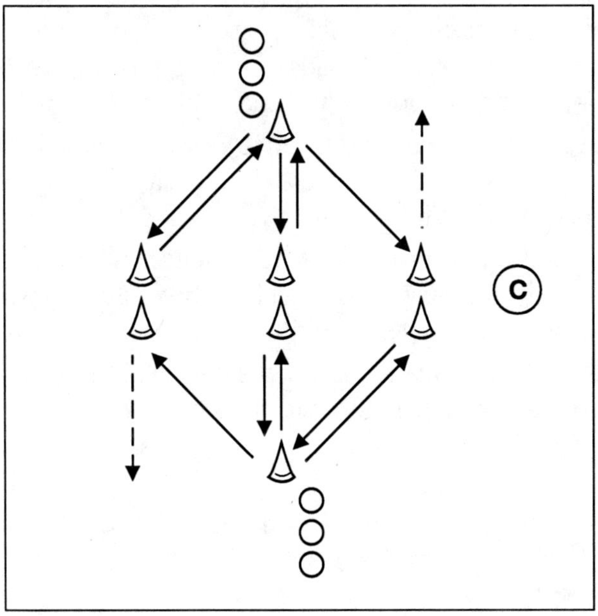

Slide-Reset Bag Drill

Nick Saban
Head Coach, University of Alabama

Objective: To develop agility and speed. Incorporated are skills related to moving quickly and efficiently in the passing pocket.

Equipment Needed: Five flat agility bags, two cones, and a football

Description:

- Align five agility bags one to one-and-a-half yards apart on a selected yard line. Place two cones three yards apart and two yards outside and five yards upfield of the outside agility bag (see the diagram).
- Position a quarterback, facing upfield and holding a football, adjacent to the first bag.
- Other quarterbacks stand adjacent to the drill area.
- The coach is aligned five yards in front of and at the midpoint of the drill area.
- On the coach's cadence, the first quarterback executes a five-step pass drop with one hitch step at the top of the pass drop. The quarterback takes a reset and laterally steps behind the first bag, slides back up past the second bag, and takes another reset lateral step in front of the second bag.
- The drill starts again on the coach's cadence with the quarterback taking a five-step pass drop with a hitch, taking a reset step laterally, sliding forward, and taking a reset step laterally past the fourth bag.
- The drill starts a third time on the coach's cadence. After the five-step pass drop, hitch, reset, and slide, the quarterback will tuck the football away and sprint through the two cones placed five yards upfield.
- The drill continues until all quarterbacks have had a sufficient number of repetitions, moving through the bags from both directions.

Coaching Points:

- Always check to see that the quarterbacks are aligned correctly and are in their proper stances before starting the drill.
- Insist that the drill be conducted at full speed.
- Instruct all quarterbacks to hold the football in the pass ready position and to always focus the eyes downfield.
- Emphasize the importance of executing the five-step drop, the hitch, the reset, and the slide correctly.
- Insist that all quarterbacks sprint through the cones as they finish the drill.

Safety Considerations:

- Proper warm-up should precede the drill.
- The drill area should be clear of all foreign articles.

Variation:

- Position a receiver downfield and have quarterbacks throw a pass on the final slide forward.

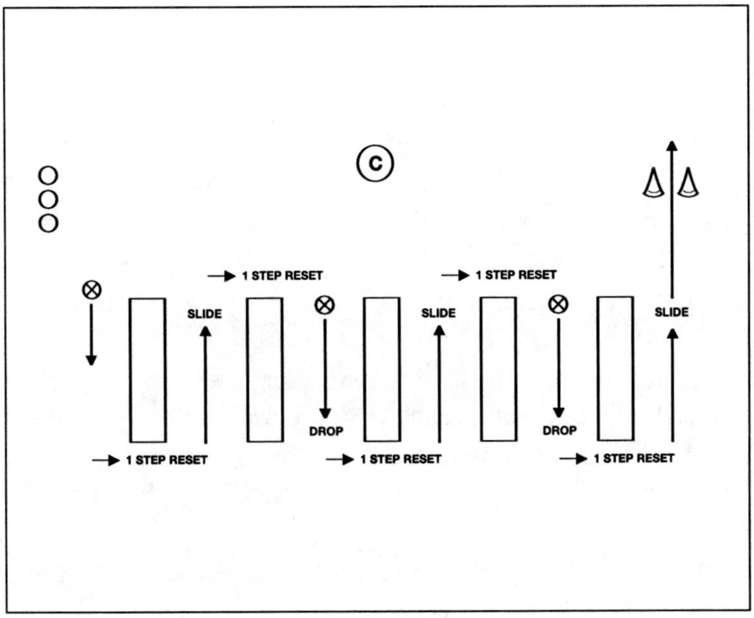

Find the Window Under Pressure Drill

Larry Wilcox
Head Coach, Benedictine College

Objective: To develop agility and speed. Incorporated are skills related to moving in the pocket and passing the football.

Equipment Needed: Footballs

Description:

- Align a quarterback, holding a football, on a selected line of scrimmage. Other quarterbacks stand adjacent to the drill area.
- Position three receivers at different pass-ending route alignments downfield. Give each of the receivers a number (1, 2, 3) (see the diagram).
- Position the coach 10 yards downfield and 10 yards in front of the quarterback. The coach keeps one hand behind his back.
- On the quarterback's cadence and snap count, the quarterback takes either a five- or seven-step pass drop.
- When the quarterback completes his pass drop, the coach signals him with his front hand to shuffle both left and right and to slide both front to back.
- From behind his back, the coach will show (at his discretion) one, two, or three fingers. The designated receiver will flash his hand, and the quarterback will pass that receiver the football.
- The drill continues until all quarterbacks have had a sufficient number of repetitions from midfield and both hash marks.

Coaching Points:

- Always check to see that all quarterbacks are in their proper stances before starting the drill.
- Insist that the drill be conducted at full speed.
- Instruct the quarterbacks to hold the football in the pass ready position throughout the drill.
- Make sure the quarterbacks keep their heads up and their eyes focused downfield at all times.
- Make sure all quarterbacks practice the proper mechanics in the throwing of all passes.

Safety Considerations:

- Proper warm-up should precede the drill.
- The drill area should be clear of all foreign articles.

Variations:

- Vary the position of the three downfield receivers.
- Incorporate pass rushers for the quarterbacks to avoid.

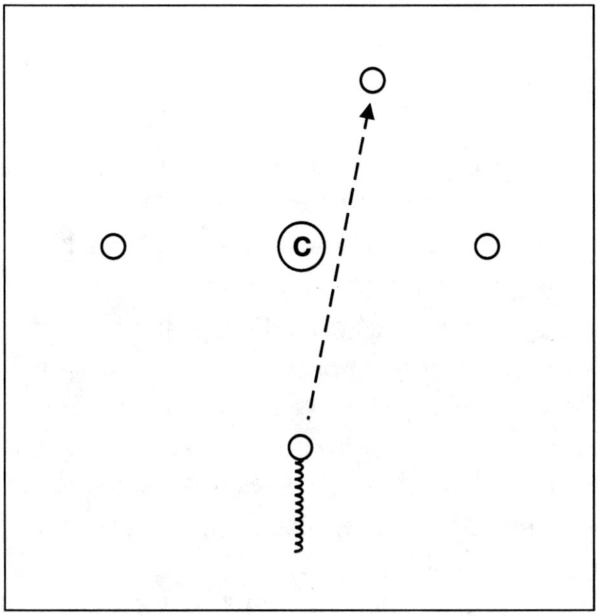

Combo Slide-Step/Forward-Back Drill

Tommy Tuberville
Head Coach, Auburn University

Objective: To develop agility and speed. Incorporated are skills related to changing directions.

Equipment Needed: Seven half-moon agility bags and a football

Description:

- Place five bags perpendicular to a selected yard line. One yard separates the first two bags. Place the next two bags one yard apart and five yards to the right of the first two bags. A fifth bag is placed five yards to the right of the middle of two bags. Position two additional bags five yards upfield and perpendicular to that yard line. Six yards separate these two bags (see the diagram).
- Position a quarterback, holding a football, beside the first bag.
- Other quarterbacks stand adjacent to the drill area.
- The coach is positioned five yards behind and at the midpoint of the drill area.
- On the coach's command, the first quarterback sprints over the first two bags, and then turns and sprints beyond and shuffles past the first downfield bag.
- The quarterback drop-steps back to the next set of bags, turns and sprints over them, and then sprints beyond and shuffles past the second downfield bag.
- The quarterback finishes the drill by drop-stepping back to the last remaining bag and turns and sprints over it.
- Drill continues until all quarterbacks have had a sufficient number of repetitions, moving from both left and right through the bags.

Coaching Points:

- Always check to see that the quarterbacks are in their proper stances before starting the drill.
- Insist that the drill be conducted at full speed.
- Instruct the quarterbacks to always carry the football at the pass ready position, with the eyes focused downfield as they move over and through the bags.

Safety Considerations:
- Proper warm-up should precede the drill.
- The drill area should be clear of all foreign articles.

Variations:
- Vary the alignment and distances between the bags.
- Have the quarterbacks finish the drill by throwing a pass to a downfield receiver.

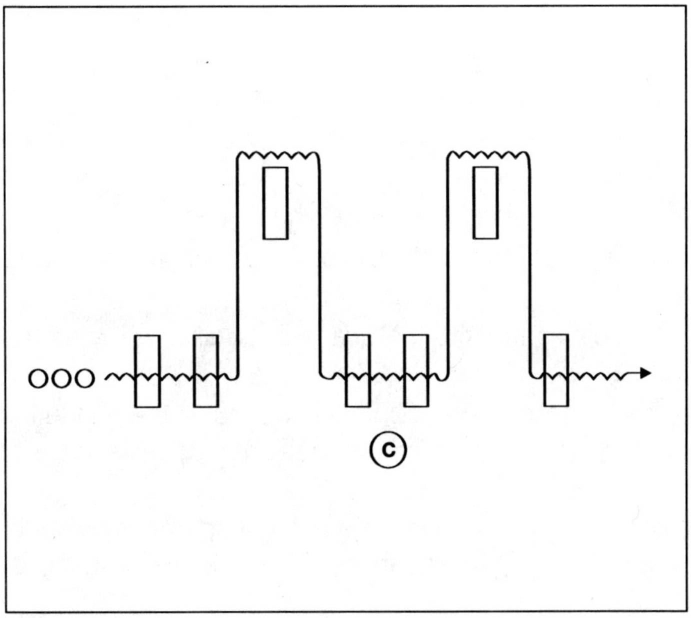

Drop and Gather Drill

Clayton Johnson *(deceased)*
Former Head Coach, Newberry College
(Drill submitted by John Bangley)

Objective: To develop agility and speed. Incorporated are skills related to moving in the passing pocket.

Equipment Needed: Four cones and footballs

Description:

- Align four cones three yards and five yards behind a selected yard line.
- A quarterback, holding a football, is positioned five yards in front of the cones and facing upfield.
- Other quarterbacks stand adjacent to the drill area.
- The coach is positioned one yard from and in a front-facing alignment to the quarterback.
- On the coach's command, the quarterback takes a five-step pass drop past the cone and gathers.
- On the coach's second command, a hand signal, the quarterback shuffles laterally (either left or right), aligning himself behind and halfway between the two outside cones on that side.
- On the coach's third command, the quarterback slides forward through the cones, then laterally (left or right), and then finishes the drill by shuffling backward between the cones.
- Drill continues until all quarterbacks have had a sufficient number of repetitions.

Coaching Points:

- Always check to see that the quarterbacks are aligned correctly and are in their proper stances before starting the drill.
- Insist that the drill be conducted at full speed.
- Emphasize the importance of always holding the football in the pass ready position.
- Instruct the quarterbacks to keep their heads up and eyes focused downfield throughout the drill.

Safety Considerations:

- Proper warm-up should precede the drill.
- The drill area should be clear of all foreign articles.

Variations:

- Vary the depth of the pass drop-steps.
- Position receivers at various alignments downfield, and have quarterbacks throw passes.

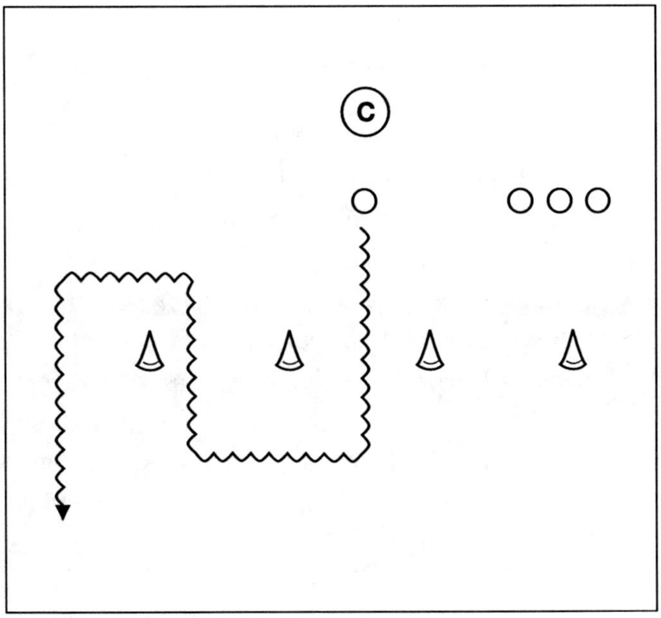

Sprint Agility Drill

Danny Hale
Head Coach, Bloomsburg University

Objective: To develop agility and speed. Incorporated are skills related to taking the proper sprint path.

Equipment Needed: Six cones and a football

Description:

- Align six cones in the proper exit-steps alignment for a designated sprint path (see the diagram).
- Position a quarterback at his standard alignment on a selected yard line.
- Other quarterbacks stand adjacent to the drill area.
- Align a receiver downfield at a designated pass-ending route.
- The coach stands in front of the drill area.
- On the coach's command, the first quarterback executes the proper exit steps around the cones, taking the quarterback to a depth of eight-and-a-half yards.
- At the designated trigger point, the quarterback passes the football to the wide receiver.
- The quarterback finishes the drill by covering for a possible interception.
- The drill continues until all quarterbacks have had a sufficient number of repetitions, moving both left and right along the sprint path.

Coaching Points:

- Always check to see that the quarterbacks are aligned correctly and in their proper stances before starting the drill.
- Insist that the drill be conducted at full speed.
- Instruct the quarterbacks as to the proper execution of the exit steps, the sprint path, and the trigger point.
- After the pass is thrown, insist that the quarterback cover for a possible interception.

Safety Considerations:

- Proper warm-up should precede the drill.
- The drill area should be clear of all foreign articles.

Variation:

- The drill can be conducted from a shotgun alignment.

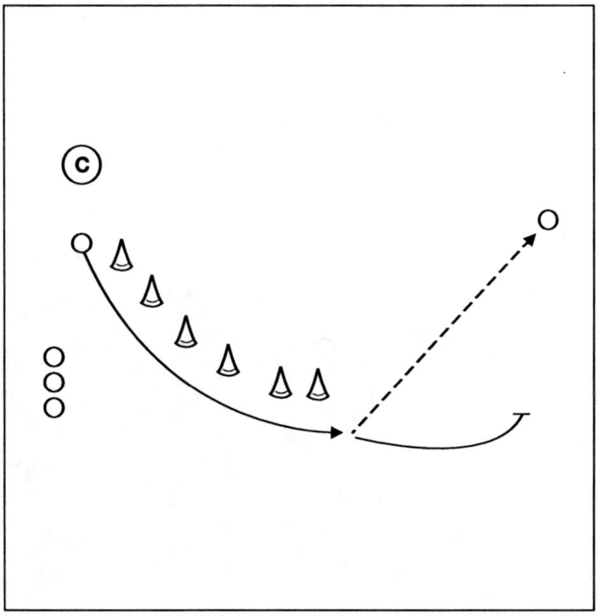

3

Offensive Line Drills

Agility Bag Drill

Randy Edsall
Head Coach, University of Connecticut

Objective: To develop agility and speed. Incorporated are skills related to body control and foot quickness.

Equipment Needed: Five agility bags and two cones

Description:

- Lay five agility bags one yard apart and perpendicular to a selected yard line.
- A cone is placed five yards from each end of the bag area (see the diagram).
- Position a row of offensive linemen two yards in front of the row of agility bags.
- The coach stands adjacent to and at the midpoint of the bags.
- This drill consists of six different movements over and through the bags—right leg hop, left leg hop, two leg hop, run through (high knees, one foot in the hole), and run through (high knees, two feet in the hole).
- On the coach's command, the first offensive lineman executes the designated movement over and through the bags.
- When the last agility bag is cleared, the offensive lineman will burst full speed past the cone at the end of the bags.
- The drill continues until all linemen have completed all the movements over and through the bags going in both directions.

Coaching Points:

- Always check to see that all offensive linemen are in their proper football ready position before starting the drill.
- Insist that the drill be conducted at full speed.
- Make sure all offensive linemen maintain the proper body alignment throughout each of the drill movements.
- Instruct the offensive linemen that on the left and right one-leg and two-leg hops, they need to get their feet back off the ground as quickly as possible.
- Instruct the offensive linemen that on the run-through (both one foot in the hole and two feet in the hole), their eyes should be focused straight ahead, arms should be pumping, and they should have a slight bend at the waist.

Safety Considerations:

- Proper warm-up should precede the drill.
- Offensive linemen with knee and ankle problems should be excused from selected movements.
- The drill area should be clear of all foreign articles.
- Alert the offensive linemen who have finished a designated movement to stay clear of the drill-finish area.

Variations:

- Use other movements over and through the bags, such as lateral runs and shuffles.
- The drill can be used as a general agility and speed drill for all positions.

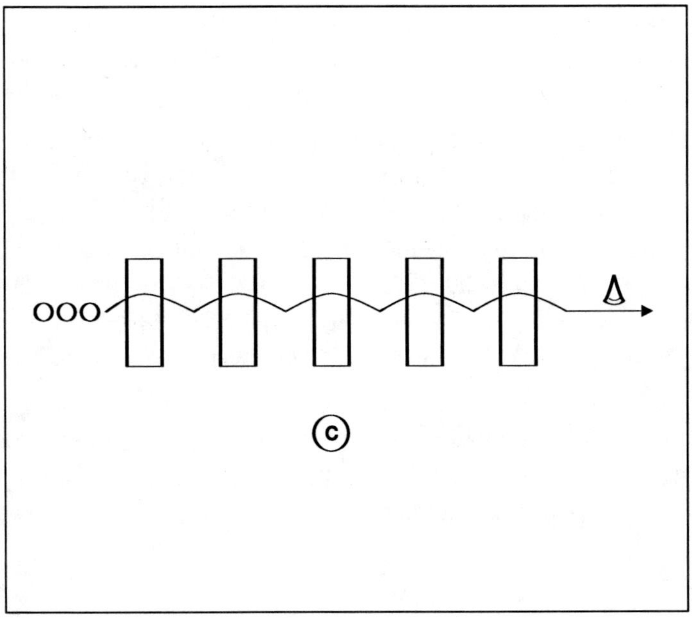

Jitterbug Drill

Ted Roof
Head Coach, Duke University

Objective: To develop agility and speed. Incorporated are skills related to execution of the punch technique used in pass protection.

Equipment Needed: Five-man blocking sled (positioned so it can move)

Description:

- Position a row of offensive linemen one yard in front of the left-most pad of a five-man blocking sled.
- The coach is positioned at various alignments adjacent to the sled.
- On the coach's command, the first offensive lineman assumes a pass-protection blocking position and strikes the first pad of the sled using the punch technique. The lineman moves to the second pad and executes the punch.
- The lineman returns to the first pad and again executes the punch. He then moves back to the second pad, delivers the punch, and then moves on to the third. He moves back to the second pad and then back to the third pad, in each case delivering the punch. After delivering the second punch to the third pad, the first offensive lineman has finished the drill.
- The second offensive lineman begins his punch technique after the first offensive lineman moves back from the third pad and delivers his punch technique on the second pad.
- After all offensive linemen have completed the punch technique, moving from the left to the right on the sled, the drill is continued with the offensive linemen moving from the right to the left on the sled.

Coaching Points:

- Always check to see that the offensive linemen are aligned correctly and are in their proper stances before starting the drill.
- Instruct the offensive linemen to use the designated punch technique and to expel air with each punch.
- Emphasize the importance of shuffling between the pads using quick feet and small steps.
- Instruct the linemen to always focus the eyes straight ahead in delivering the punch.
- In executing the punch, instruct the linemen to stagger-step as each punch is executed.

Safety Considerations:

- Proper warm-up should precede the drill.
- Insist that the drill be conducted at full speed.
- Instruct the linemen as to the proper techniques of executing the punch technique.
- The sled should be checked periodically for possible maintenance and repairs.

Variations:

- The drill can be used with the linemen executing the punch with one hand.
- The drill can be used with players holding a medicine ball as a substitute for the pad on the sled.

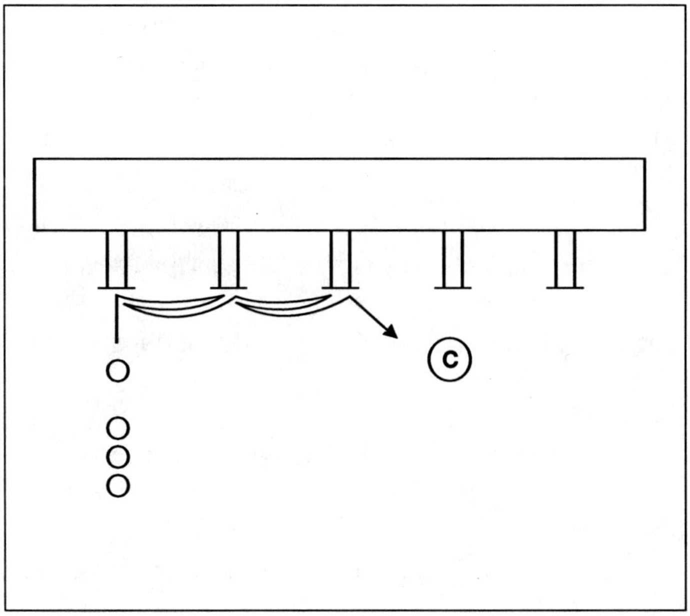

Duck Walk Drill

Urban Meyer
Head Coach, University of Florida

Objective: To develop general agility and flexibility.

Equipment Needed: Four cones

Description:

- Place four cones 10 yards apart to form a square. Cones are designated A, B, C, and D (see the diagram).
- Position a row of offensive linemen adjacent to cone A.
- The coach is positioned at various points in and around the square.
- On the coach's command, the first offensive lineman executes a forward duck walk from cone A to cone B.
- When the offensive lineman passes cone B, he executes a lateral duck walk to cone C.
- After passing cone C, the lineman executes a backyard duck walk past cone D.
- After passing cone D, the lineman will finish the drill by executing a second lateral duck walk back past cone A.
- Drill continues until all linemen have had a sufficient number of repetitions.

Coaching Points:

- Instruct all offensive linemen as to the proper method of executing the forward, backward, and lateral duck walks by maintaining a chest up-shoulders back posture, while keeping the elbows tight to the ribs.
- Instruct the linemen that they should face in the same direction throughout the four phases of the drill.
- Insist that the linemen finish the drill by duck walking past cone A.

Safety Considerations:

- Proper warm-up should precede the drill.
- Offensive linemen with hip, knee, and ankle problems should be excused from the drill.
- Alert offensive linemen who are waiting to perform the drill to stay clear of the drill-finish area.

Variations:

- The drill can be used as a general agility and flexibility drill for all positions.
- The drill can be used as a reaction drill without using cones, with the coach signaling the different duck walk directions.

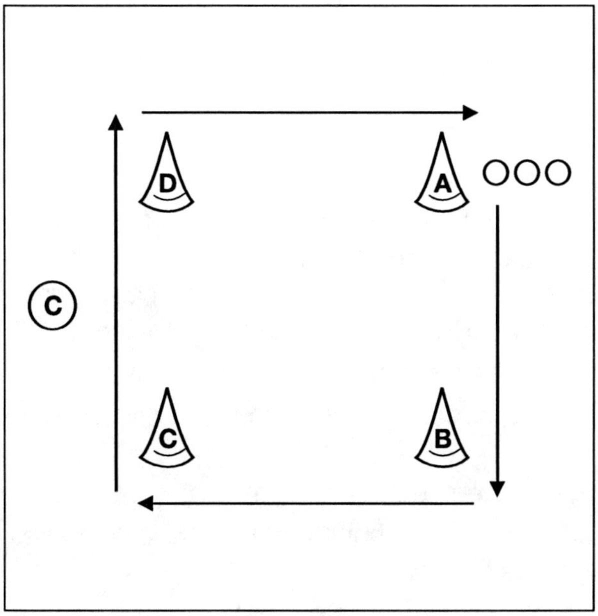

Mirror Dodge Drill

Jack Henry
Assistant Coach, San Diego Chargers

Objective: To develop agility and speed. Incorporated are skills related to the execution of the punch technique used in pass protection.

Equipment Needed: Two cones

Description:

- Place two cones one to one-and-a-half yards apart on a selected yard line.
- Position a pair of front-facing linemen at the midpoint of the two cones. One lineman is designated the offensive lineman and the other the pass rusher (the rabbit). The offensive lineman places his heels on the yard line between the cones and protects an imaginary pass pocket (see the diagram).
- Other offensive linemen stand adjacent to the drill area.
- Position the rabbit at arms length away from and directly in front of the offensive lineman.
- The coach stands adjacent to the drill area.
- On the coach's first command, both the offensive lineman and the rabbit assume the football ready position.
- On the coach's second command, the rabbit can move from side-to-side, can spin, can stop and start, or stop and change direction.
- The offensive lineman mirrors the rabbit movements with every directional change as the offensive lineman maintains his pass pro position with the heels in the front of the line.
- During the 5- to 10-second duration of the drill, the rabbit is allowed to advance forward only two times.
- When the rabbit moves forward, the offensive lineman moves from his pass pro position and executes the punch technique.
- If the rabbit should get past the punch of the offensive lineman, the rabbit returns to the start position and the drill is restarted.
- The drill continues until all offensive linemen have had a sufficient number of repetitions.

Coaching Points:

- Always check to see that the offensive linemen and the rabbit are in the proper football ready position before starting the drill.

- Insist that the drill be conducted at full speed.
- Insist that offensive linemen maintain their pass pro position throughout the drill.
- Make sure the arms-length distance between the rabbit and the offensive lineman is maintained throughout the drill, except on the two times the rabbit is allowed to advance toward the pass pocket.
- Instruct the offensive linemen that the only time they can use the punch technique is when the rabbit changes his side-to-side movements and attacks the pass pocket (physical contact can only take place at this time).
- Emphasize the importance of maintaining the heels of the offensive linemen on the front of the yard line between the two cones at all times.

Safety Considerations:

- Proper warm-up should precede the drill.
- Shoulder pads and a helmet with its chinstrap snapped should be worn with this drill.
- Instruct the offensive linemen as to the proper technique of mirroring the rabbit in executing the punch technique.

Variations:

- Change the time of the duration of the drill.
- The drill can be made competitive by keeping score between the rabbit successes and that of the offensive linemen.
- Use linebackers and defensive backs as rabbits to increase the speed of the drill.

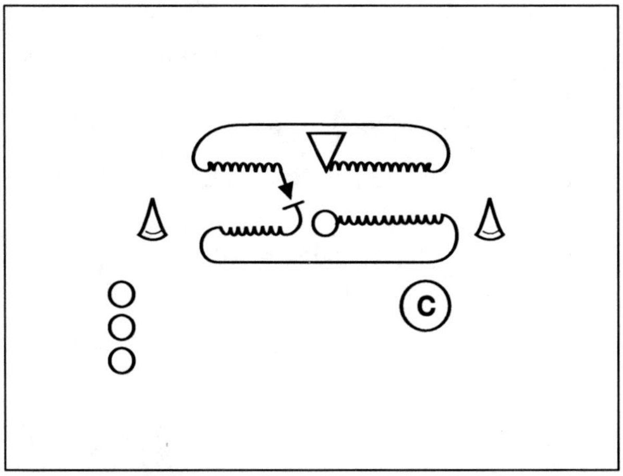

Four-Corner Square-In Drill

Bobby Lamb
Head Coach, Furman University

Objective: To develop speed and agility. Incorporated are skills related to changing directions.

Equipment Needed: Five cones

Description:

- Place four cones 10 yards apart to form a square. Cones are designated A, B, C, and D. A fifth cone is placed seven yards from and beside cone A (see the diagram).
- Position a row of offensive linemen adjacent to the fifth cone.
- The coach is aligned between and adjacent to cones A and D.
- On the coach's first command, the first offensive lineman assumes the football ready position.
- On the coach's second command, the offensive lineman backpedals past cone A. He then turns and sprints around cone B.
- The lineman now backpedals past cone C and then completes the drill by sprinting past cone D.
- The drill continues until all drill participants have had a sufficient number of repetitions, starting from both the right and left sides of the cones.

Coaching Points:

- Always check to see that the offensive linemen are in the football ready position before starting the drill.
- Insist that the drill be conducted at full speed.
- Instruct the offensive linemen as to the desired techniques of sprinting and backpedaling.
- Emphasize the importance of maintaining a low center of gravity and changing direction quickly.
- Insist that the offensive linemen sprint past the last cone in finishing the drill.

Safety Considerations:

- Proper warm-up should precede the drill.
- The drill area should be clear of all foreign articles.

Variations:

- The drill can be used as a general speed and agility drill for all positions.
- Substitute other movements for the sprint and backpedal, such as sideways shuffle and carioca.

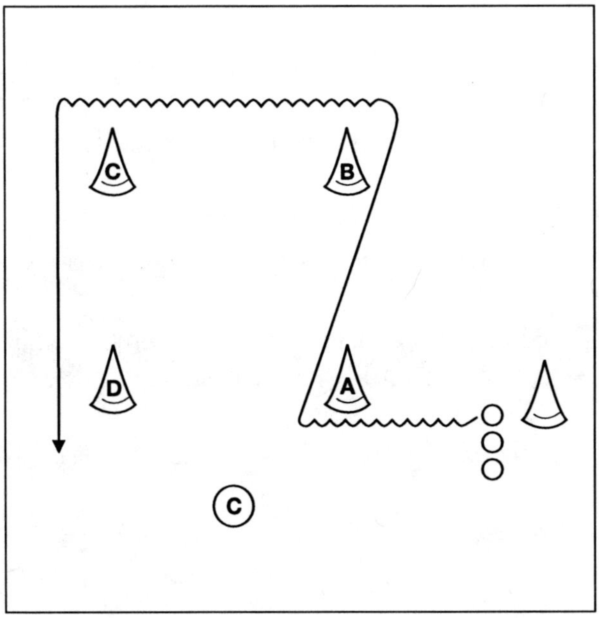

Shuffle Drill

Pride Ratteree
Former Assistant Coach, University of South Carolina
(Drill submitted by Dale Steele)

Objective: To develop general agility and speed. Incorporated are skills related to maintaining the proper football position.

Equipment Needed: Five half-moon agility bags and two cones

Description:

- Lay five-half moon agility bags three yards apart and perpendicular to a selected yard line. Place a cone five yards outside both ends of the bags (see the diagram).
- Align a row of offensive linemen adjacent to the cone at either end of the row of agility bags.
- The coach is positioned adjacent to the drill area.
- On the coach's first command, the first offensive lineman assumes the football ready position.
- On the coach's second command, the offensive lineman shuffles to the far end of the first agility bag, plants his outside foot, and shuffles to the far end of the second bag.
- At the end of the second bag, the lineman plants his outside foot and shuffles to the third bag.
- This sequence is followed until the offensive lineman reaches the end of the fifth bag.
- The offensive lineman now finishes the drill by sprinting past the cone placed five yards beyond the last bag.
- The drill continues until all offensive linemen have had a sufficient number of repetitions, moving both left and right through the bags.

Coaching Points:

- Check to see that all offensive linemen are in the proper football ready position before the second command is given.
- Insist that the drill be conducted at full speed.
- Instruct the offensive linemen to execute the shuffle correctly and to drive hard off the outside-foot plant at the end of each bag.
- Emphasize the importance of maintaining the proper weight distribution throughout the shuffle and focusing the eyes straight ahead.
- Insist that the offensive linemen finish the drill by sprinting past the cone on that side.

Safety Considerations:

- Proper warm-up should precede the drill.
- Instruct the offensive linemen as to the proper execution of the shuffle.

Variations:

- The drill can be used as a general agility and speed drill for all positions.
- Vary the distances between the agility bags.

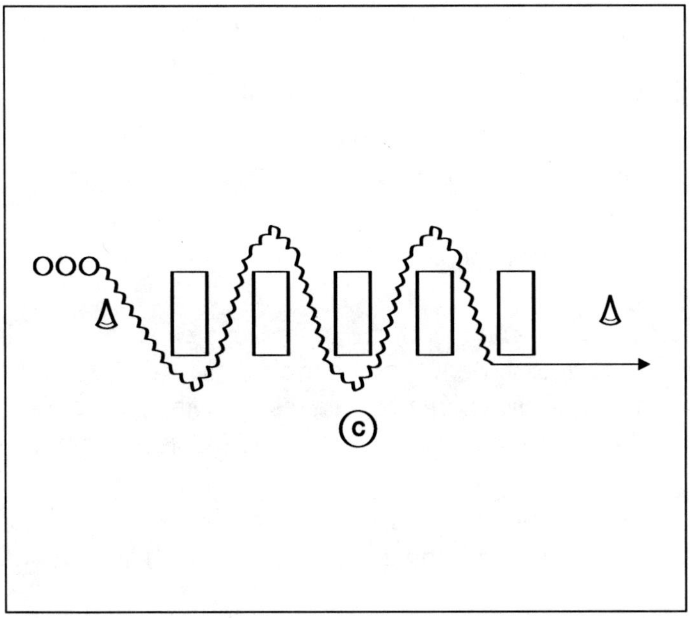

Duck Demeanor Drill

Louis Clyburn
Former Assistant Coach, Elon University

Objective: To develop general agility and flexibility.

Equipment Needed: Six half-moon agility bags and a cone.

Description:

- Lay six half-moon agility bags two yards apart and perpendicular to a selected yard line. A cone is placed three yards outside and adjacent to the top of the last bag (see the diagram).
- Position a row of offensive linemen adjacent to and in a sideways alignment to the bottom of the first agility bag (see the diagram).
- The coach stands adjacent to the drill area.
- On the coach's first command, the offensive lineman assumes the Duck Demeanor position.
- On the coach's second command, the offensive lineman moves laterally past and around the first bag, and then moves backward past and around the end of the second bag. The offensive lineman continues this lateral and backward movement around the bags, while maintaining the Duck Demeanor position through and around all the bags.
- The drill continues until all offensive linemen have had a sufficient number of repetitions, moving from both the left and right through and around the bags.

Coaching Points:

- Always check to see that all offensive linemen are in the correct Duck Demeanor position.
- Insist that the drill be conducted at as full speed as possible.
- Instruct the offensive linemen as to the proper techniques of executing the Duck Demeanor position (hips low, chest straight and up, weight on the insides of the feet, elbows locked in tight to the waist, and eyes focused straight ahead).

Safety Considerations:

- Proper warm-up should precede the drill.
- Instruct the offensive linemen as to the proper technique of moving from the Duck Demeanor position.

Variations:

- Vary the distance between the agility bags.
- Use other duck movements through and around the bags, such as moving laterally.

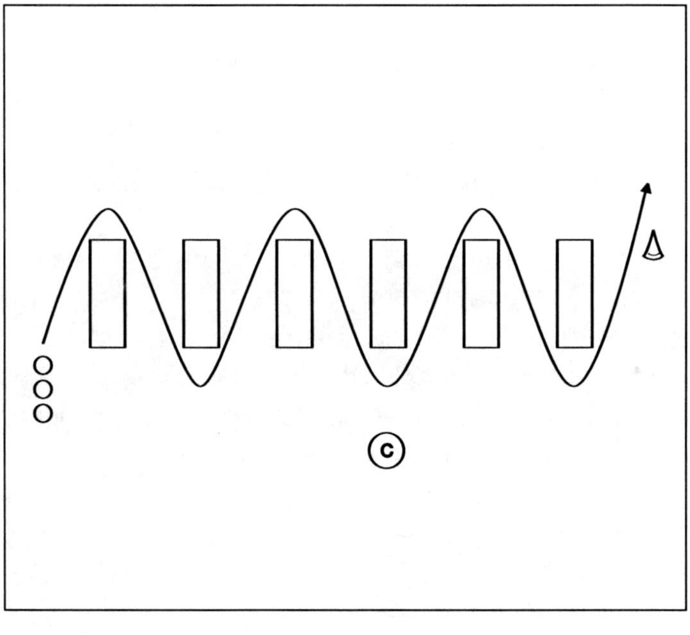

Pen Racing Drill

Bobby Bowden
Head Coach, Florida State University

Objective: To develop general agility and speed. Incorporate are skills related to the execution of different movement patterns.

Equipment Needed: One pen 10 yards long, five yards wide, four feet high, and made of two-by-four boards and wire mesh

Description:

- Align two rows of offensive linemen side-by-side and adjacent to the end of the pen.
- The coach is positioned adjacent to the drill area.
- On the coach's first command, the first two offensive linemen assume the football ready position.
- On the coach's second command, the two offensive linemen race under and through the pen in the football ready position.
- The drill continues until all offensive linemen have had a sufficient number of repetitions, racing under and through the pen in the football ready position.
- The drill can incorporate other movement patterns, racing under and through the pen (racing backward, sideways, and on all fours).

Coaching Points:

- Always make sure that the offensive linemen start the drill in the correct position.
- Insist that the drill be conducted at full speed.
- Instruct the linemen as to the proper techniques in executing the different movement patterns.

Safety Considerations:

- Proper warm-up should precede the drill.
- The pen should be checked periodically for possible maintenance and repairs.
- Helmets should be worn with the chinstraps snapped.

Variations:

- The drill can be used as a general agility and speed drill for all positions.
- Position a blocking dummy at the end of the pen, and have linemen execute shoulder blocks at the end of the drill.

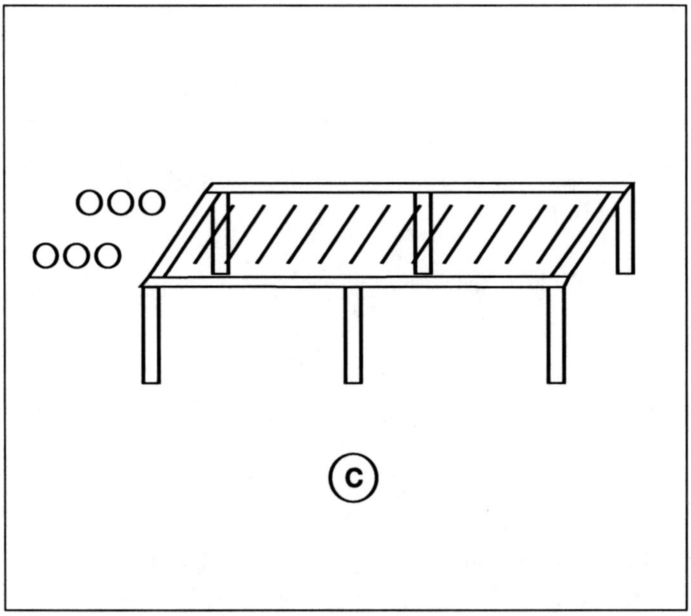

Movement Wave Drill

Rich Skrosky
Assistant Coach, Elon University

Objective: To develop general agility and speed. Incorporated are skills related to the execution of the pass block.

Equipment Needed: Grid-line boxes five-yards-by-five-yards

Description:

- Draw four five-yard-by-five-yard grid boxes with the base of the grid boxes on a sideline (see the diagram).
- Position five offensive linemen with their inside foot on the corners of the grid boxes that form the base of the grid. All offensive linemen face a goal line.
- Other linemen line up behind the first row of offensive linemen (see the diagram).
- The coach is positioned five yards in front of the drill area.
- On the coach's first command, the first row of linemen assume the perfect pass-protection position.
- On the coach's second command, "Kick" or "Power," the linemen executes the designated movement with the accompanying slide movement (the kick movement is always a quick side step away from the center with the outside foot, and the power movement is a quick step with the inside foot back toward the center. The kick or power step is quickly followed by a quick slide movement with the opposite foot in the same direction as the kick or power movement.
- The coach pauses slightly after each command as he changes up the kick or power and slide movements.
- The drill duration is six to eight seconds, with the coach directing the offensive linemen to sprint upfield five yards to finish the drill.
- The drill continues until all drill participants have had a sufficient number of repetitions.

Coaching Points:

- Always check to see that the offensive linemen are in the perfect pass-protection position with the outside foot stagger, feet spread apart wider than the hips, and knees inside of the feet before starting the drill.
- Insist that the drill be conducted at full speed.
- Instruct all offensive linemen to establish a big chest, with the hands up and open, and the elbows slightly bent.

- On the kick command, instruct the offensive linemen to move the outside foot diagonally to the outside followed by a quick slide with the opposite foot also to the outside.
- On the power command, instruct the offensive linemen to move the inside foot diagonally to the inside followed by a quick slide with the opposite foot also to the inside.
- Emphasize the importance of always maintaining perfect pass-protection position throughout the drill.
- Insist that the offensive linemen sprint five yards upfield in finishing the drill.

Safety Considerations:

- Proper warm-up should precede the drill.
- The drill area (including the sideline area) should be clear of all foreign articles.

Variations:

- Use visual commands as well as verbal commands.
- Have offensive linemen go one at a time.

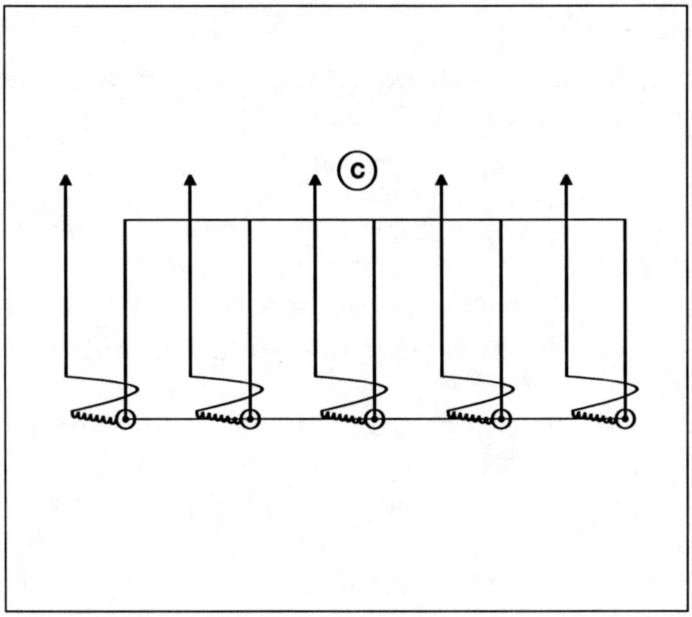

Wheel Drill

Skip Holtz
Head Coach, East Carolina University

Objective: To develop general agility and speed.

Equipment Needed: Five half-moon agility bags

Description:

- Place four agility bags in a four-spoke wheel alignment. A fifth bag is placed horizontally five yards in front of the wheel alignment (see the diagram).
- Position a row of offensive linemen adjacent to the drill area and facing the fifth bag on the opposite side of the drill area.
- The coach is aligned adjacent to the drill area.
- On the coach's first command, the first lineman positions himself in a four-point stance with his hand in the hub of the wheel and the feet between the spokes.
- On the coach's second command, the lineman moves in a clockwise direction chopping his feet, while moving over, through, and around the bags.
- When the lineman gets back to the starting position, he stands up and sprints to and over the fifth bag.
- Drill continues until all linemen have had a sufficient number of repetitions, moving in both a clockwise and counter-clockwise direction.

Coaching Points:

- Always check to see that the offensive linemen are in the correct four-point stance before starting the drill.
- Insist that the drill be conducted at full speed.
- Instruct the linemen that the hands must always be positioned on the ground and inside the hub of the wheel.
- In moving over and through the bags, instruct the linemen not to cross the feet, click the heels, or touch the bags.
- Emphasize the importance of keeping the head up and not letting the knees touch the ground.
- Insist that the linemen finish the drill by sprinting over the bag on the far side of the wheel alignment.

Safety Considerations:

- Proper warm-up should precede the drill.
- Players with knee or ankle problems should be excused from the drill.

Variation:

- The drill can be used as a general agility and speed drill for all positions.

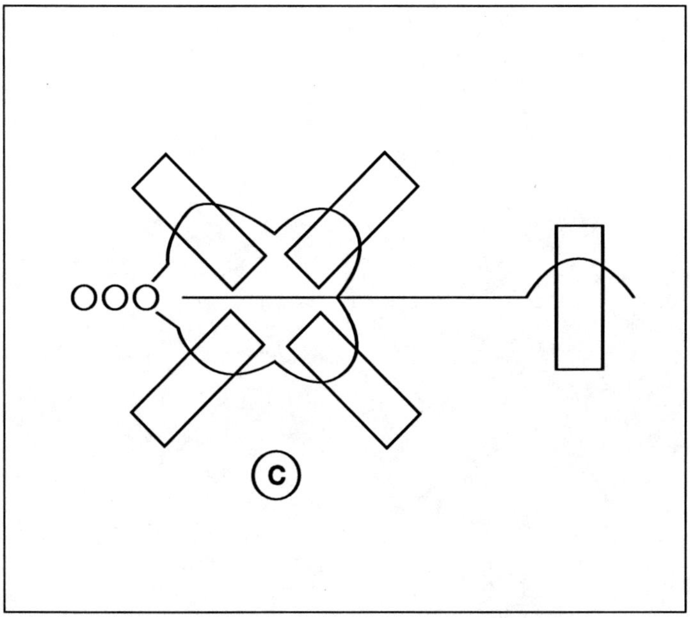

4

Wide Receiver Drills

Four Cone Drill

Charlie Weis
Head Coach, Notre Dame

Objective: To develop general agility and speed. Incorporated are skills related to planting and coming out of a pass route, breaks, and catching the football.

Equipment Needed: Four cones and four footballs

Description:

- Place four cones (A, B, C, and D) 10 yards apart to form a square (see the diagram).
- Position a row of wide receivers adjacent to cone A.
- The coach is positioned in the middle of the square with four footballs.
- On the coach's first command, the first receiver assumes the designated stance.
- On the coach's second command, the receiver runs to cone B as the coach passes him the football at the halfway point between cones A and B. After catching the football, the receiver drops the caught pass before he reaches cone B.
- After passing cone B, the receiver sprints cone C as the coach again passes him the football at the halfway point between the cones B and C. After catching the football, the receiver again drops the caught pass before reaching cone C.
- The receiver repeats the previous step between cones C and D.
- After passing cone D, the receiver sprints back toward cone A as the coach passes the football to him at the halfway point between cones D and A.
- After catching the fourth pass thrown by the coach, the receiver finishes the drill by sprinting past cone A.
- The drill continues until all wide receivers have had a sufficient number of repetitions.
- The drill should be conducted in both clockwise and counter-clockwise directions.

Coaching Points:

- Always check to see that the wide receivers are in their proper stances before starting the drill.
- Insist that the drill be conducted at full speed.
- Emphasize the importance of looking the football into the hands with every caught pass.
- The coach should throw a variety of passes—high balls, low balls, and balls behind the receiver.

Safety Considerations:

- Proper warm-up should precede the drill.
- The drill area should be clear of all foreign articles.
- Alert wide receivers who are waiting to perform the drill to stay clear of the drill-finish area.
- Instruct the wide receivers after catching the football to always drop the caught football away from the drill area.

Variations:

- The drill can be used by all pass-receiving positions.
- Vary the distance between the cones.

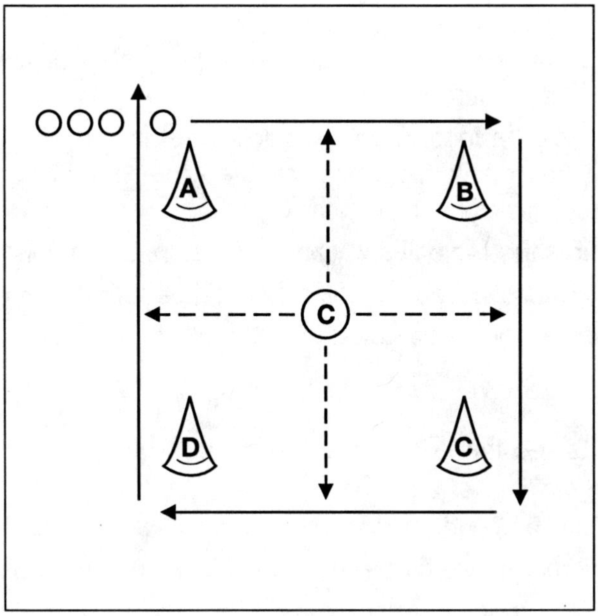

Quick Turn/Quick Feet Drill

Stan Hixon
Assistant Coach, Washington Redskins

Objective: To develop general agility and speed. Incorporated are skills related to making quick in and out cuts when receiving a pass.

Equipment Needed: Two cones and four footballs

Description:

- Align a row of wide receivers on a selected yard line just inside the onside field numbers.
- A coach (passer), holding the football, is positioned on the near hash marks (see the diagram).
- On the coach's command ("Go"), the first wide receiver drives out of his stance and runs a four-step quick-out route.
- The receiver drops the football on the sideline, returns to the playing field, sprints upfield seven yards, plants his outside foot, executes the hook route, and catches the second pass thrown by the coach.
- The receiver tucks the football away and sprints upfield to finish the drill.
- The drill continues until all wide receivers have had a sufficient number of repetitions.
- The drill is reversed, being executed in the opposite direction.

Coaching Points:

- Always check to see that all wide receivers are aligned correctly and are in their proper stances.
- Insist that the drill be conducted at full speed.
- Emphasize the importance of executing the quick out and hook route correctly.
- In catching the out route, instruct the wide receivers to catch the football over the right shoulder and keep both feet inbounds by tapping the lead foot and dragging the back foot.
- Emphasize the importance of snapping the head around and catching the pass with the hands.
- Insist that the receivers sprint upfield 10 yards after catching the hook pass.

Safety Considerations:

- Proper warm-up should precede the drill.
- The drill area (especially the sideline area) should be clear of all foreign articles.
- It is imperative that a player (manager) be stationed on the sideline to retrieve the football dropped by the receiver and return it to the coach.

Variations:

- The drill can be used by all pass-receiving positions.
- The drill can be used with a variety of wide-receiver patterns.

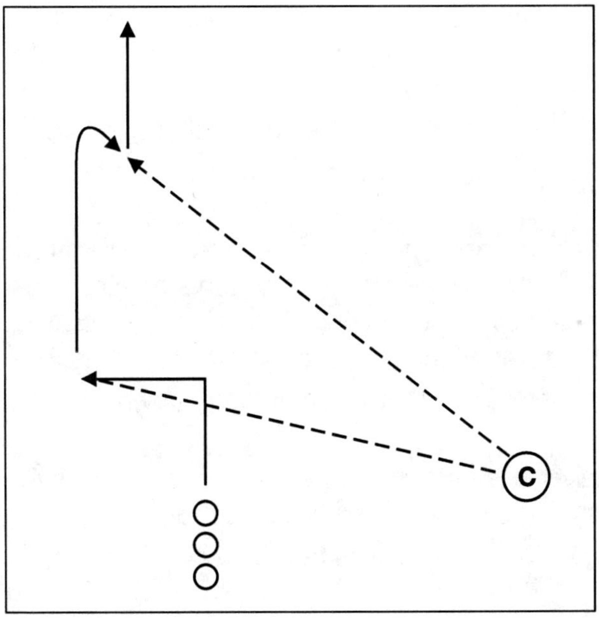

"M" Drill

Shane Montgomery
Head Coach, Miami University (Ohio)

Objective: To develop general agility and speed. Incorporated are skills related to making sharp cuts and catching a thrown pass.

Equipment Needed: Five cones and a football

Description:

- Place three cones (A, B, and D) five yards apart to form two sides of a five-yard square. A fourth cone (C) is placed below and between cones B and D to form the letter M. A fifth cone (E) is placed one yard from and at an angle to cone D (see the diagram).
- Position a row of wide receivers behind and outside cone A.
- The coach, holding a football, is positioned two yards below the midpoint of the letter M.
- On the coach's command, the first wide receiver drives from stance and sprints toward cone B. As the receiver passes cone B he throttles down, plants his outside foot, and turns and sprints past cone C. As he passes cone C, he again throttles down, plants his outside foot, turns, and sprints past cone D.
- As the receiver passes cone D, he again throttles down, plants his outside foot, and runs past cone E.
- When the receiver passes cone E, the coach passes the football to the receiver, who catches the football, turns, and sprints upfield
- The drill continues until all receivers have had a sufficient number of repetitions.

Coaching Points:

- Always check to see that all wide receivers are in their proper stances when starting the drill.
- Insist that the drill be conducted at full speed.
- Instruct the wide receivers when throttling down to lower their hips, keep their shoulder over the knees, plant their outside foot, and cut sharply before sprinting to the next cone.
- Insist that the wide receivers turn and sprint upfield 10 yards after catching the pass.

Safety Considerations:

- Proper warm-up should precede the drill.
- The drill area should be clear of all foreign articles.

Variations:

- The drill can be used by all pass-receiving positions.
- The drill can be set up and performed in the opposite direction.

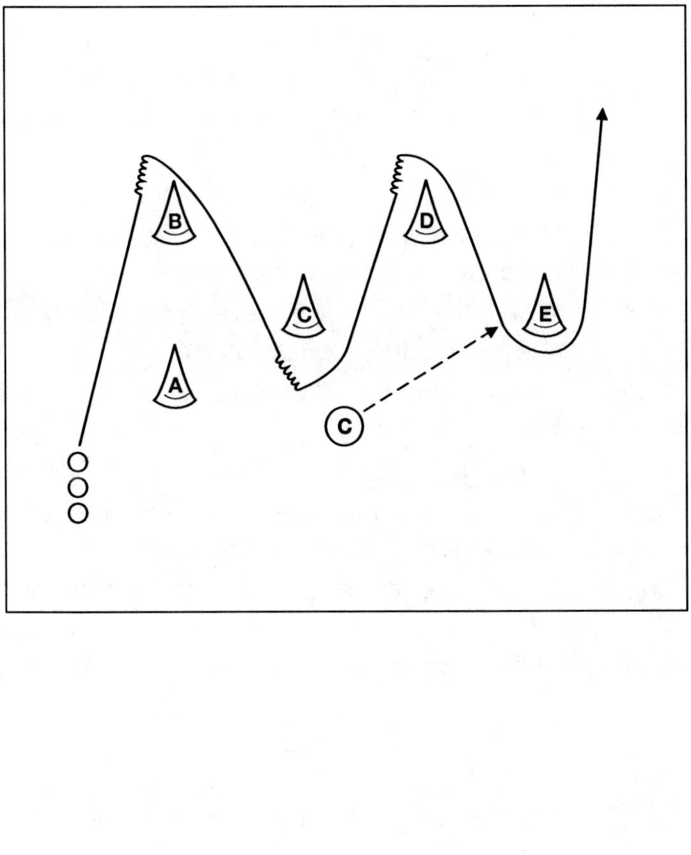

Acceleration Drill

Tommy West
Head Coach, University of Memphis

Objective: To develop general speed and agility. Incorporated are skills related to acceleration, quickness, and cutting after catching a thrown pass.

Equipment Needed: One pop-up dummy, two cones, and a football

Description:

- Place a pop-up dummy on the nearside hash mark on a selected yard line. Place a cone 10 yards beyond the pop-up dummy on the same yard line. A second cone is placed at a 90-degree angle and five yards downfield from the first cone (see the diagram).
- Position a row of receivers behind the pop-up dummy.
- The coach, holding a football, is positioned 10 yards below the selected yard line and midway between the pop-up dummy and the first cone.
- On the coach's command, the first wide receiver explodes from his stance and executes a release move around the pop-up dummy.
- After the release move is executed, the receiver sprints to the cone, while maintaining his run down the yard line.
- As the receiver approaches the cone, the coach passes the football to him.
- After catching the football, the receiver passes the cone, plants his outside foot, makes a 90-degree cut, and sprints upfield to the second cone.
- When reaching the upfield cone, the receiver makes a significant cut and sprints 10 yards to finish the drill.
- The drill continues until all wide receivers have had a sufficient number of repetitions.

Coaching Points:

- Always check to see that the wide receivers are in their proper stances in starting the drill.
- Insist that the drill be conducted at full speed.
- Make sure the wide receivers execute the selected release technique correctly.
- Insist that the receivers maintain their run down the yard line after executing their releases.
- Instruct the wide receiver to tuck the football away after catching the pass.

- When approaching the second cone, have the receiver square up and picture himself breaking a tackle or faking out the defender as he moves around the cone.
- Insist that the receiver sprints downfield 10 yards after cutting off the second cone.

Safety Considerations:
- Proper warm-up should precede the drill.
- The drill area should be clear of all foreign articles.
- Players with knee or ankle problems should be excused from the drill.

Variations:
- The drill can be used for all pass-receiving positions.
- Vary the distances between the pop-up dummy and the cone or between the two cones.
- Reverse the direction of the drill by moving the two cones and the coach to the opposite side.
- Position a manager/coach at the second cone, and have receivers beat the coach.

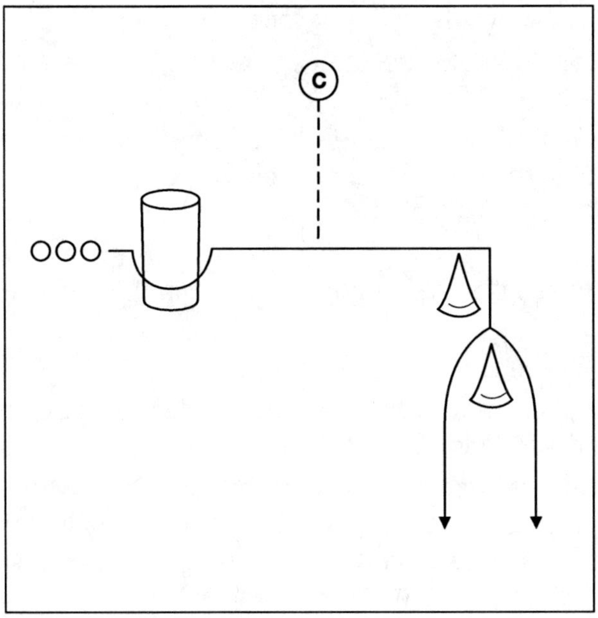

Route Technique Drill

Rich Brooks
Head Coach, University of Kentucky

Objective: To develop general agility and speed. Incorporated are skills related to running pass routes correctly and catching the football.

Equipment Needed: Ten cones and two footballs

Description:

- Align 10 cones in the following pattern. Place the first five cones in a zigzag pattern three yards apart and at a 45-degree angle to each other. The next four cones should be placed five yards apart and at a 90-degree angle to one another. The final cone is placed five yards downfield from the last cone (see the diagram).
- Position a row of wide receivers at either end of the drill area.
- A coach, holding a football, is positioned at the far end of the drill area. A second coach is positioned adjacent to the middle of the drill area.
- On the coach's command ("Ready, go"), the first wide receiver drives from his stance and runs through the maze of cones.
- After moving past the last cone, the wide receiver catches the football thrown by the coach positioned at the end of the drill and sprints upfield.
- Drill continues until all wide receivers have had a sufficient number of repetitions in moving through the cones from both directions.

Coaching Points:

- Always check to see that the wide receivers are in their proper stances in starting the drill.
- Insist that the drill be conducted at full speed.
- When running through the cones set at a 45-degree angle, insist that the wide receivers keep their heads up, maintain a low center of gravity, plant off the outside foot, and keep the eyes focused straight ahead with their arms pumping.
- When making the 90-degree cuts, instruct the receivers to concentrate on using the correct technique instead of running at full speed, sink the hips, and keep the eyes focused straight ahead with arms pumping.
- Insist that the receiver sprints upfield 10 yards after catching the football.

Safety Considerations:

- Proper warm-up should precede the drill.
- The drill area should be clear of all foreign articles.

Variations:

- The drill can be used for all pass-receiving positions.
- Vary the distances between the cones.

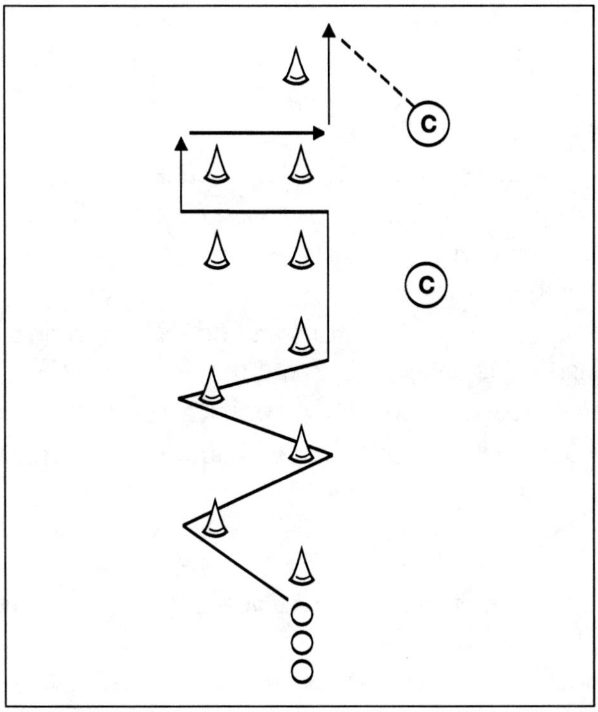

Concentration Drill

Fred Goldsmith
Head Coach, Lenoir Rhyne College

Objective: To develop general agility and speed. Incorporated are skills related to hand-eye coordination, maintaining body control, and changing directions.

Equipment Needed: Three cones and a tennis ball

Description:

- Align three cones (A, B, and C) in the shape of the letter L, with cones A and B placed in a vertical plane eight yards apart. Cone C is placed in a horizontal plane four yards from cone B (see the diagram).
- Position a row of wide receivers just inside of cone A.
- The coach, holding a tennis ball, is positioned outside of cone A.
- On the coach's command, the first wide receiver drives from his stance and sprints to—and circles around—cone B.
- The wide receiver sprints to and circles around cone C, sprints back past cone B, makes a 90-degree cut, and sprints to the outside of cone A.
- As the receiver approaches cone A, the coach tosses him the tennis ball.
- The drill continues until all receivers have had a sufficient number of repetitions from both a left and a right alignment.

Coaching Points:

- Always check to see that the wide receivers are in their correct stances before starting the drill.
- Insist that the drill be conducted at full speed.
- Instruct the wide receivers to circle the cones with small quick steps while keeping a low center of gravity.
- Emphasize the importance of maintaining a forward body lean with eyes focused straight ahead when sprinting between the cones.
- Insist that the receivers accelerate out of each break and sprint 10 yards upfield after catching the tossed tennis ball.

Safety Considerations:

- Proper warm-up should precede the drill.
- The drill area should be clear of all foreign articles.

Variations:

- The drill can be used for all pass-receiving positions.
- Vary the distances between the cones.

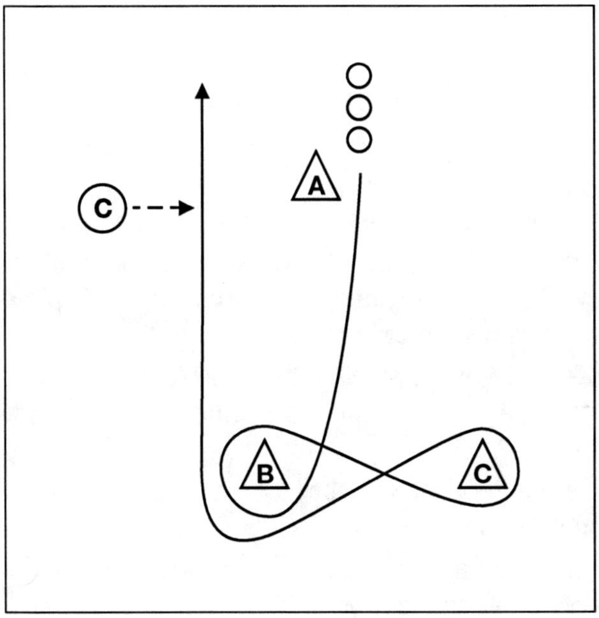

Agility Shuttle Drill

Les Miles
Head Coach, Louisiana State University

Objective: To develop general agility and speed. Incorporated are skills related to catching the football.

Equipment Needed: Two cones and footballs

Description:

- Align two cones (A and B) 10 yards apart on a selected yard line.
- Position a row of wide receivers behind cone A.
- The coach, holding a football, is aligned seven yards from and at the midpoint of the two cones (see the diagram).
- On the coach's command, the first receiver drives from his stance and runs to cone B.
- At some point during the run, the coach passes the football to the wide receiver, who secures the football and continues his run to cone B, places the football near cone B, and redirects his run back to cone A.
- The coach passes a second football to the wide receiver, who catches the football. He continues to cone A, places the football near cone A, and again redirects his run to cone B.
- The coach passes the receiver a football for the third time, and the receiver redirects his run and sprints 10 yards upfield.
- The drill continues until all receivers have had a sufficient number of repetitions, starting from both a left and right alignment.

Coaching Points:

- Always check to see that the wide receivers are in their correct stances before starting the drill.
- Insist that the drill be conducted at full speed.
- Emphasize the urgency of redirecting as the receivers move from one cone to the other.
- Instruct the wide receivers to look the football into their hands with each catch.
- Insist that the wide receivers sprint 10 yards upfield after catching the third pass.

Safety Considerations:

- Proper warm-up should precede the drill.
- The drill area should be clear of all foreign articles.

Variations:

- The drill can be used for all pass-receiving positions.
- Vary the distance between the cones.

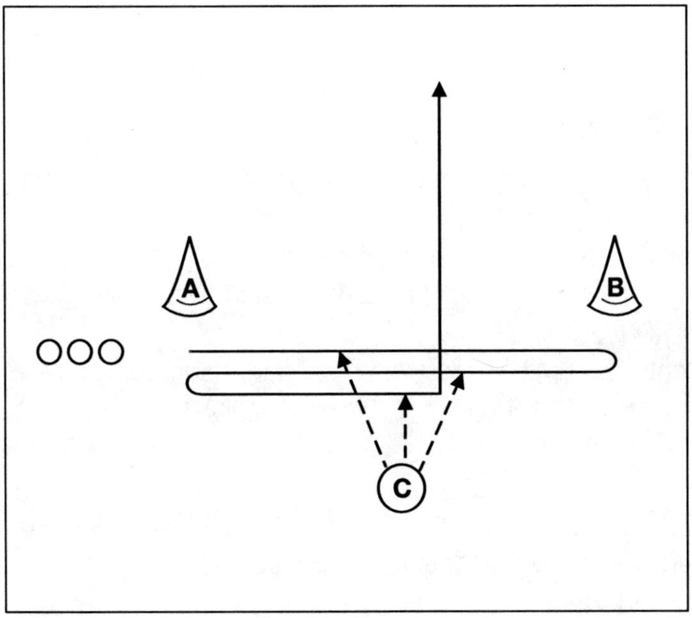

Carioca Flip Drill

Mark Snyder
Head Coach, Marshall University

Objective: To develop general agility and speed. Incorporated are skills related to improving footwork, running precision pass routes, and catching the football.

Equipment Needed: Four cones and footballs

Description:

- Place four cones (A, B, C, and D) five yards apart to form a square on a selected yard line.
- Position a row of wide receivers adjacent to cone A.
- A coach (passer), holding a football, is positioned at the midpoint of the base of the square.
- On the coach's command, the first receiver cariocas past cone B, plants the outside foot, and runs the ending steps of the designated pass route: hitch, dig, curl, or out (see the diagram).
- The drill continues until all receivers have had a sufficient number of repetitions from both a left and right receiver/quarterback alignment.

Coaching Points:

- Make sure all wide receivers perform the carioca movement correctly.
- Insist that the drill be conducted at full speed.
- Instruct the wide receivers to always perform the carioca movement facing the opposite way that the pass route is to be completed (which is the flip part of the drill).
- Instruct all wide receivers as to the proper techniques of performing the carioca, of planting the outside foot, and the flip at the end of the carioca.
- Make sure that all receivers secure the football after the catches are made and finish the drill by sprinting upfield.

Safety Considerations:

- Proper warm-up should precede the drill.
- The drill area should be clear of all foreign articles.

Variations:

- The drill can be used for all pass-receiving positions.
- Vary the distances between the cones.

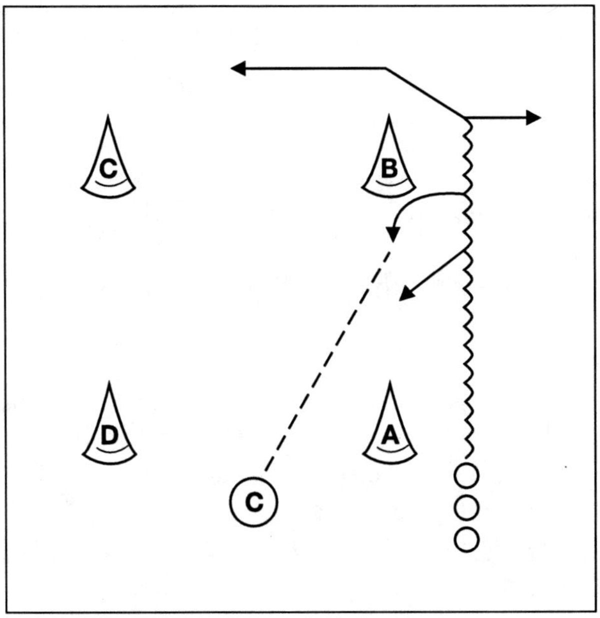
C
B
D
A
C

Buckeye Shuffle Burst Drill

Jeff Uhlenhake
Assistant Coach, Ohio State University

Objective: To develop general agility and speed. Incorporated are skills related to running a precision pass route and catching the football.

Equipment Needed: Four half-moon agility bags, four cones, and footballs

Description:

- Place four half-moon agility bags three feet apart and perpendicular to a selected yard line. Place cones A and B three yards outside and adjacent to the top of the four bags. Cones C and D are placed 10 yards upfield and in the same vertical plane as cones A and B (see the diagram).
- Align a row of wide receivers in a football ready position adjacent to cone A and facing the row of bags.
- Other wide receivers stand adjacent to the drill area.
- The coach, holding a football, is positioned at the midpoint and five yards behind the bag area.
- On the coach's command, the first wide receiver assumes the football ready position and shuffles laterally around and through the bag.
- After the wide receiver has passed cone B, he plants his right foot, makes a 90-degree cut, accelerates, and sprints to cone C.
- At cone C, the wide receiver can execute one of five designated pass-ending routes (out, cross, post, curl, or corner) and catches the football thrown by the coach (see the diagram).
- The drill continues until all receivers have had a sufficient number of repetitions, moving from both left and right around and through the bags.

Coaching Points:

- Always check to see that the wide receivers assume the football ready position before the start of the drill.
- Insist that the drill be conducted at full speed.
- Instruct the wide receivers as to the correct techniques for the execution of the shuffle.
- Instruct the wide receivers as to the correct techniques for executing the five pass-ending routes.
- When executing the designated pass route, make sure the wide receivers plants off the appropriate foot and accelerates into each pass cut.

Safety Considerations:

- Proper warm-up should precede the drill.
- The drill area should be clear of all foreign articles.

Variation:

- The drill can be used for all pass-receiving positions.

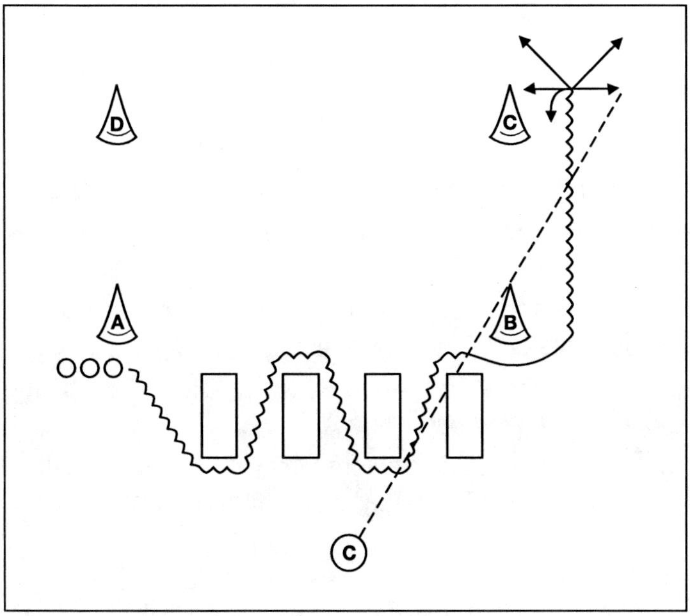

Cone Drill

Les Miles
Head Coach, Louisiana State University

Objective: To develop general agility and speed. Incorporated are skills related to making a 90-degree cut.

Equipment Needed: Four cones

Description:

- Place four cones (A, B, C, and D) five yards apart to form a square (see the diagram).
- Align a row of wide receivers behind and outside of cone A.
- The coach stands three yards behind and at the midpoint between cones A and B.
- On the coach's command, the first wide receiver drives from his stance and sprints to cone B.
- After passing cone B, the wide receiver executes a three-step breakdown, plants the outside foot, makes a 90-degree angle cut, and sprints to cone C.
- The previous description is performed at cones C and D, and the wide receiver finishes the drill by sprinting past cone A.
- The drill continues until all wide receivers have had a sufficient number of repetitions, starting from both a left and a right alignment.

Coaching Points:

- Always check to see that the wide receivers are in their proper stance before starting the drill.
- Insist that the drill be conducted at full speed.
- Instruct the wide receivers to lower their center of gravity and to maintain the proper body alignment as they execute the 90-degree cuts.
- Emphasize the importance of pumping the arms and focusing the eyes straight ahead throughout the drill.

Safety Considerations:

- The drill area should be clear of all foreign articles.
- Alert the wide receivers who are waiting to perform the drill to stay clear of the drill-finish area.

Variations:

- The drill can be used by all pass-receiving positions.
- The drill can be used as a general agility and speed drill for all positions.

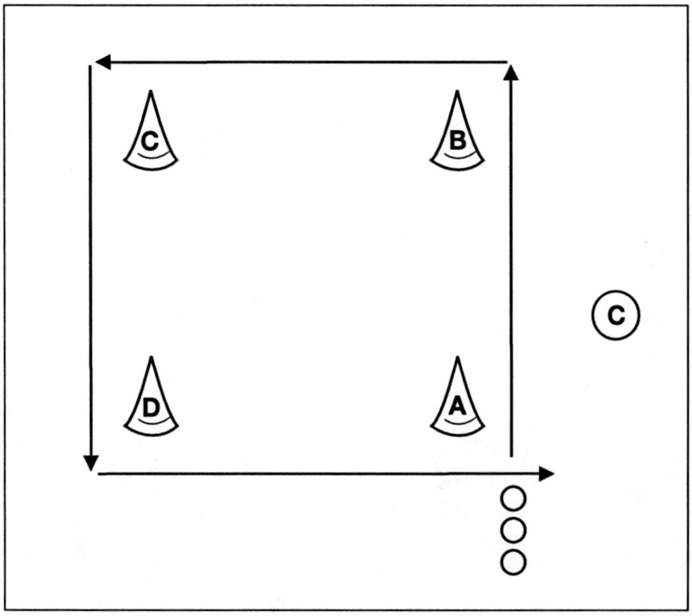

5

Tight End Drills

Tennis Ball Drop and Toss Drill

Joe Rudolph
Assistant Coach, University of Nebraska

Objective: To develop general agility and speed. Incorporated are skills related to concentration.

Equipment Needed: Two cones and tennis balls

Description:

- Place two cones in a vertical alignment, one on the goal line and the other on the 10-yard line. Any two yard lines can be used. (see the diagram).
- Position a row of tight ends behind and adjacent to the cone on the goal line.
- The coach, with two tennis balls in hand, is positioned at the three-yard line.
- On the coach's command ("Go"), the first tight end explodes from his stance as the coach drops the tennis ball from his hand, which is extended out at eye level.
- The tight end must tap the tennis ball before it completes its second bounce.
- After tapping the tennis ball away, the tight end proceeds past the second cone as the coach tosses the second tennis ball directly over the tight end's head.
- The tight end must chase down and catch the second tennis ball before it completes its second bounce.
- The drill continues until all tight ends have completed a sufficient number of repetitions.

Coaching Points:

- Always check to see that the tight ends are in their proper stances before starting the drill.
- Insist that the drill be conducted at full speed.
- Instruct the tight ends to explode from their stances, and to keep their shoulders low as they reach for and tap the first tennis ball.
- Emphasize the importance of running through the first tennis ball's drop and tap, and chasing down and catching the second tennis ball.

Safety Considerations:

- Proper warm-up should precede the drill.
- The drill area should be clear of all foreign articles.
- The coach and players must help in retrieving all tennis balls.

Variations:

- The drill can be used for all pass-receiving positions.
- Place a stand-up dummy in front of the tight ends as they drive out of their stances, and have them work on inside and outside line release.
- The drill can be used as a linebacker and defensive back drill.

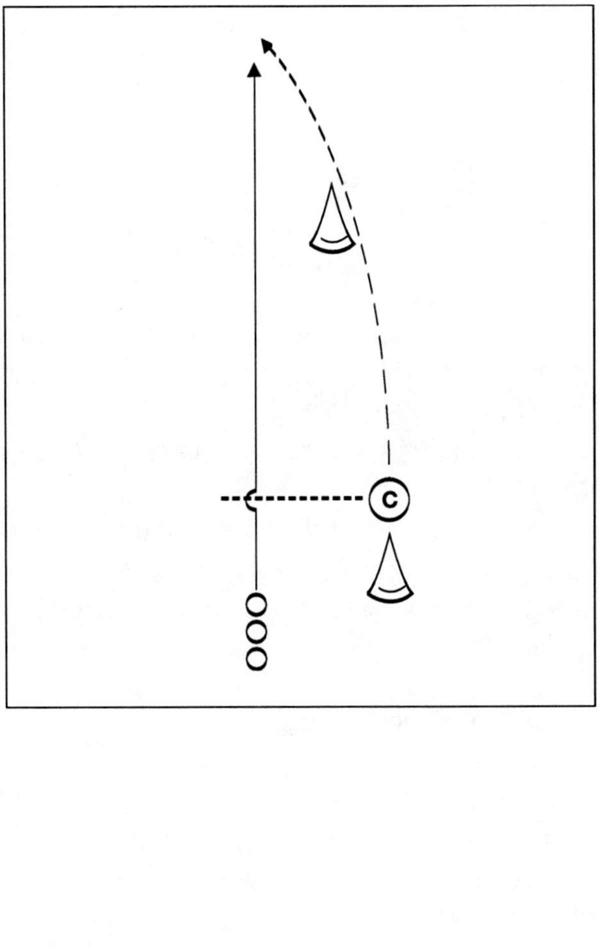

Cone Break Drill

Trent Walters
Assistant Coach, Philadelphia Eagles

Objective: To develop agility and speed. Incorporated are skills related to catching the football.

Equipment Needed: Four cones and two footballs

Description:

- Place four cones (A, B, C, and D) in a rectangular alignment with a width of 10 yards and a height of eight yards (see the diagram).
- Position a row of tight ends adjacent to cone A.
- The coach, holding a football, is positioned three yards behind and three yards outside cone D.
- On the coach's command, the first tight end drives from his stance and runs at half to three-quarter speed to cone B. When the tight end passes cone B, he executes a 90-degree cut and proceeds to cone C.
- After he passes cone C, the tight end executes another 90-degree cut as the coach passes him the football.
- The tight end catches the football, tucks it away, and sprints past cone D.
- The drill continues until all tight ends have had a sufficient number of repetitions, from both a left and right tight-end-to-passer play relationship.

Coaching Points:

- Always check to see that all tight ends are in their proper stances before starting the drill.
- Make sure all tight ends maintain the proper body alignment throughout the drill.
- Emphasize the importance of maintaining the proper forward body lean and keeping eyes focused straight ahead throughout the drill.
- Instruct the tight ends to always lower the center of gravity and to plant the outside foot when making all 90-degree cuts.
- Insist that all tight ends look the pass into their hand and tuck it away quickly.

Safety Considerations:

- The drill area should be clear of all foreign articles.
- Alert drill participants who have completed the drill to stay clear of drill-finish area.

Variations:

- The drill can be used by all pass-receiving positions.
- The drill can be used as a linebacker and defensive back drill.

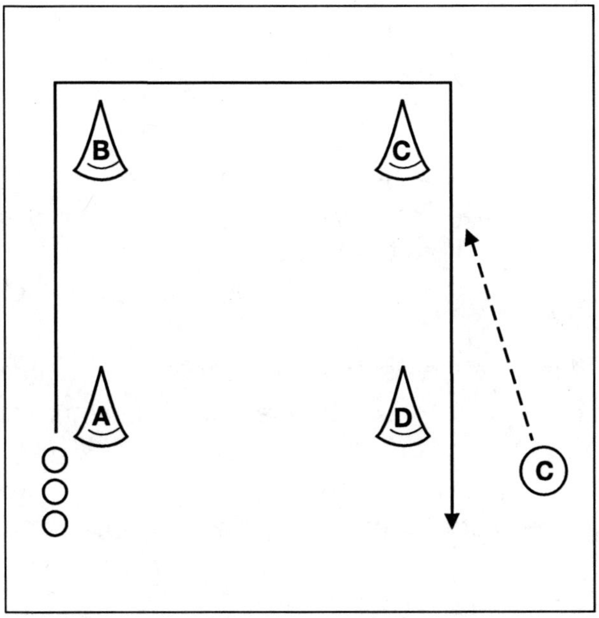

Cone Drill

Mark Richt
Head Coach, University of Georgia

Objective: To develop general speed and agility. Incorporated are skills related to catching the football.

Equipment Needed: Nine cones and footballs

Description:

- Place five cones five yards apart down a sideline. Place four additional cones two-and-a-half yards from and splitting the distance between the five cones on the sideline (see the diagram).
- Position a row of tight ends at one end of the cone area.
- Position a coach, holding a football, adjacent to and 10 yards in front of the cone and at the opposite end from the tight ends.
- On the coach's command, the first tight end drives out of his stance and sprints through and around each cone.
- As the tight end reaches the last cone, he catches the pass thrown by the coach.
- The drill continues until all tight ends have had a sufficient number of repetitions.

Coaching Points:

- Always check to see that all tight ends are in their proper stances before starting the drill.
- The drill should be conducted at full speed.
- Instruct all tight ends to make their cuts on the outside the cones.
- Emphasize the importance of maintaining proper body alignment, planting the outside foot, and pumping the arms as the tight end sprints through and around the cones.
- Insist that all tight ends look the thrown pass into their hands and tuck it away as quickly as possible.

Safety Considerations:

- Proper warm-up should precede the drill.
- The drill area (especially the sideline areas) should be clear of all foreign articles.

Variations:

- The drill can be used by all pass-receiving positions.
- The drill can be used as a linebacker and defensive back drill.
- Vary the distances between the cones, both in depth and width.

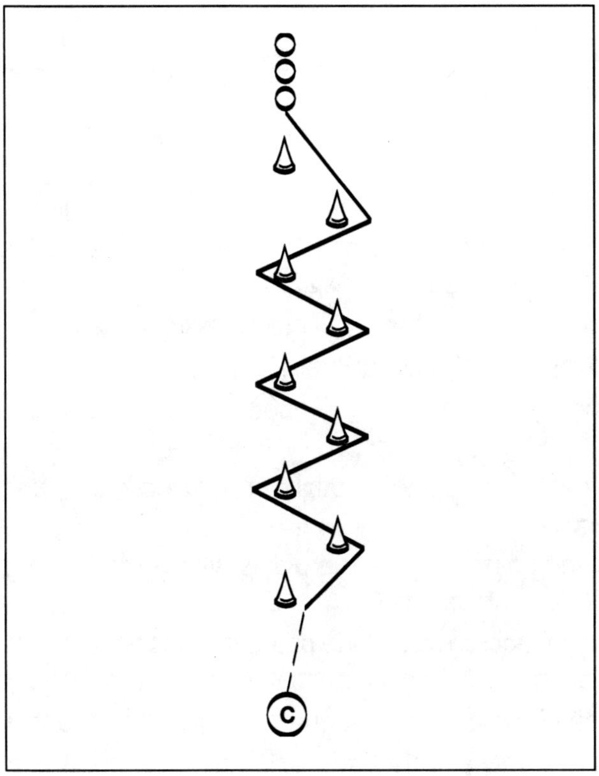

Buckeye Carioca Burst Drill

Jim Tressel
Head Coach, The Ohio State University

Objective: To develop general agility and speed. Incorporated are skills related to running a precision pass route and catching the football.

Equipment Needed: Four half-moon agility bags, four cones, and footballs

Description:

- Place four half-moon agility bags three feet apart and perpendicular to a selected yard line. Place cones A and B three yards outside and adjacent to the top of the four bags. Cones C and D are placed 10 yards in upfield and in the same vertical plane as cones A and B (see the diagram).
- Align a tight end in a football ready position, facing cone A.
- Other tight ends stand adjacent to the drill area.
- The coach, holding a football, is positioned at the midpoint and five yards behind the bag area.
- On the coach's command, the first tight end cariocas over and through the bags and past cone B.
- After the tight end passes cone B, he plants his right foot and makes a 90-degree cut and accelerates and sprints to cone C.
- At cone C, the tight end executes one of the five designated pass routes (out, cross, post, curl, or corner) as the coach passes the football to the tight end.
- After catching the football, the tight end turns and sprints upfield for 10 yards.
- The drill continues until all tight ends have had a sufficient number of repetitions, moving both left and right over the bags.

Coaching Points:

- Always check to see that the tight ends assume the proper football ready position before starting the drill.
- Insist that the drill be conducted at full speed.
- Instruct the tight end as to the correct technique in the execution of the carioca.
- When executing the designated pass route, make sure the tight end plants off the outside foot and accelerates into each pass cut.
- Insist that the tight ends finish the drill by turning upfield and sprinting 10 yards after catching the thrown pass.

Safety Considerations:

- Proper warm-up should precede the drill.
- The drill area should be clear of all foreign articles.

Variation:

- The drill can be used for all pass-receiving positions.

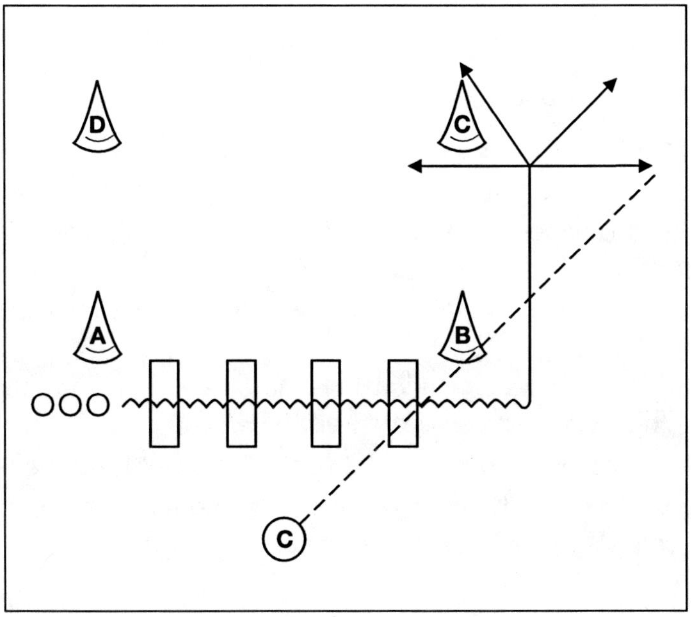

Cones and Catch Drill

Mike Sheppard
Assistant Coach, Cincinnati Bengals

Objective: To develop agility and speed. Incorporated are skills related to catching and securing the football.

Equipment Needed: Ten cones and footballs

Description:

- Place four cones (A, B, C, and D) two yards apart to form a square.
- Position a row of tight ends adjacent to cone A (see the diagram).
- The coach, holding a football, is aligned five yards downfield and adjacent to cone D.
- On the coach's cadence and snap count, the first tight end drives from his stance and runs past cone B.
- When the first tight end passes cone B, he plants his outside foot and runs past cone C.
- After passing cone C, the tight end plants the outside foot and sprints toward the coach who throws him an above-the-waist pass.
- The tight end catches the pass, tucks it away, and sprints past the coach.
- Drill continues until all drill participants have had a sufficient number of repetitions, moving in both directions around the cones.

Coaching Points:

- Always check to see that the tight ends are in their proper stances before starting the drill.
- Insist that the drill be conducted at full speed.
- In running through and around the cones, emphasize the importance of always planting the outside foot, keeping a low center of gravity when rounding the cone, and accelerating to the next cone.
- Instruct the tight ends, when catching the football, to secure the football and tuck it away quickly.
- Insist that the tight end sprints past the coach after catching the football.

Safety Considerations:

- Proper warm-up should precede the drill.
- The drill area should be clear of all foreign articles.

Variations:

- Add a 360-degree spin after the tight end rounds cone C and before the coach passes the tight ends the football.
- The drill can be used for all pass-receiving positions.
- The drill can be used as a linebacker and defensive back drill.

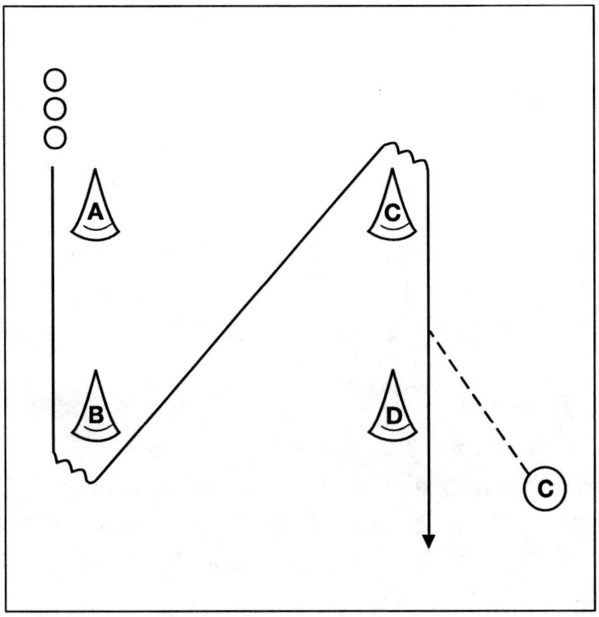

Four Corner Drill

Bob Ford
Head Coach, University of Albany

Objective: To develop agility and speed. Incorporated are skills related to catching the football

Equipment Needed: Four dots, two cones, and footballs

Description:

- Align four dots 10 yards apart to form a square. Align a cone five yards outside and five yards below each of the dots that forms the base of the square (see the diagram).
- Align a row of tight ends adjacent to the dot that forms the right bottom of the square.
- Position a coach at the midpoint two yards behind the two dots that form the base of the square. A second coach, holding a football, is positioned five yards behind the first coach.
- On the front coach's command, the first tight end sprints to the middle of the square, faces the coach, and fires his feet.
- The front coach points to one of the four dots, while also giving one of three verbal commands (sprint, backpedal, or shuffle). The tight end carries out the command in the direction of the indicated dot, and then waits for the coach's next hand signal and verbal command.
- After each tight end is given five or six commands, the coach yells, "Out," and the tight end sprints to the nearest outside cone and catches the football thrown by the second coach.
- The drill continues until all tight ends have had a sufficient number of repetitions.

Coaching Points:

- Always check to see that all tight ends are in the football ready position, firing their feet as they reach the center of the square.
- The drill should be conducted at full speed.
- Emphasize the importance of maintaining the proper body alignment throughout the drill.
- Instruct the tight ends to always move in a straight line when reacting to the commands from the front coach.
- Insist that the tight ends, after catching the pass, finish the drill by sprinting past the cone.

Safety Considerations:

- Proper warm-up should precede the drill.
- The drill area should be clear of all foreign articles.
- Alert the tight ends waiting to perform the drill to stay clear of the drill-finish area.

Variations:

- Vary the distance between the dots.
- The drill can be used for all pass-receiving positions.
- Have drill participants recover or fumble instead of catching a thrown pass when finishing the drill.
- The drill can be used as a linebacker and defensive back drill.

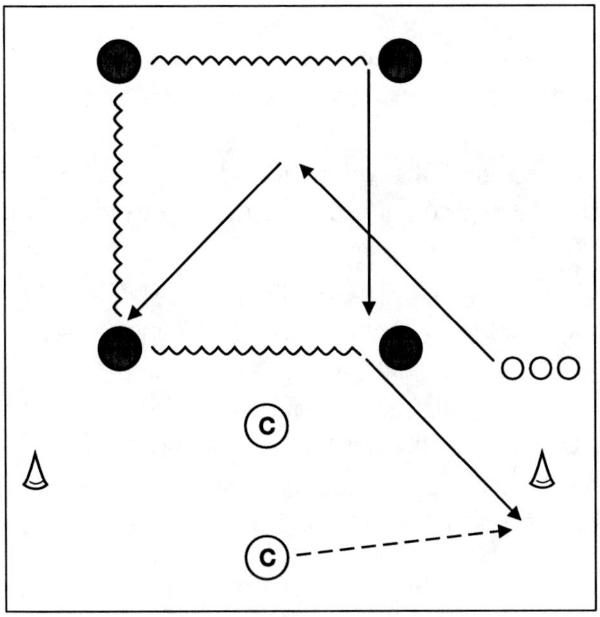

Release and Route Drill

Kirk Ferentz
Head Coach, University of Iowa

Objective: To develop agility and speed. Incorporated are skills related to catching the football.

Equipment Needed: A hand shield, four cones, and footballs

Description:

- Align four cones (A, B, C, and D) five yards apart to form a square. The base of the square is on a selected yard line (see the diagram).
- A defender holding a hand shield is positioned five yards below and to the left of cone A.
- Position a row of tight ends in front of the defender.
- The coach, holding a football, is positioned five yards below and at the midpoint of the base of the square.
- On the coach's command, the first tight end explodes from his stance, executes the designated release technique on the defender holding the shield, and then drives to cone A.
- After passing cone A, the tight end plants the left foot and sprints past cone B.
- After passing cone B, the tight end sprints past cone C, plants the right foot, and sprints to cone D.
- After passing cone D, the tight end plants the left foot, cuts at a 90-degree angle, sprints upfield, and catches the pass thrown by the coach.
- The drill continues until all tight ends have had a sufficient number of repetitions, moving from both sides of the base of the square.

Coaching Points:

- Always check to see that the tight ends are in their proper stances before starting the drill.
- Insist that the drill be conducted at full speed.
- Instruct the tight ends to always plant the outside foot and to keep a low center of gravity as they move around each cone.
- Make sure that the tight ends accelerate to the next cone after each 90-degree cut.
- Emphasize the importance of getting in and out of the cuts as quickly as possible.
- In finishing the drill, insist that the tight ends sprint 10 yards downfield after catching the pass.

Safety Considerations:

- Proper warm-up should precede the drill.
- The drill area should be clear of all foreign articles.

Variations:

- Vary the distance between the cones.
- The drill can be used for all pass-receiving positions.

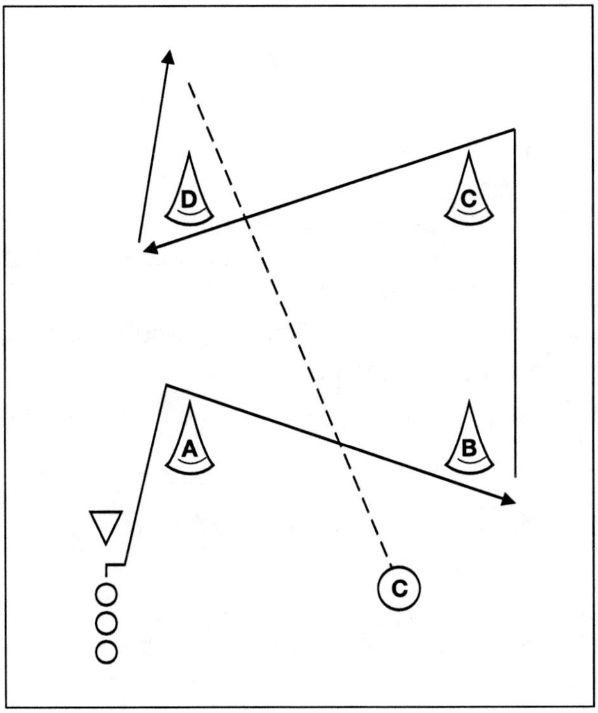

Four-and-Two Drill

Clarence Stasavich *(deceased)*
Former Head Coach, East Carolina University
(Drill submitted by David Alexander)

Objective: To develop agility and speed. Incorporated are skills related to catching the football.

Equipment Needed: Footballs

Description:

- Align tight ends in a row and perpendicular to a selected yard line.
- A coach (passer), holding a football, is positioned 15 yards in front of the first tight end (see the diagram).
- On the coach's command, the first tight end assumes the football ready position.
- On the coach's ball signal (shows pass), the first tight end takes four quick steps forward and two quick steps backward, and then cuts at a 90-degree angle either left or right on the coach's shoulder turn.
- The coach passes the football to the tight end, who makes the reception, sprints to the coach, and gives him the football.
- The drill continues until all tight ends have had a sufficient number of repetitions.

Coaching Points:

- Make sure that the tight ends are in the football ready position before starting the drill.
- Insist that the drill be conducted at full speed.
- Instruct the tight ends to keep their heads up and eyes focused on the passer throughout the drill.

Safety Considerations:

- Proper warm-up should precede the drill.
- The drill area should be clear of all foreign articles.

Variations:

- The drill can be used for all pass-receiving positions.
- The drill can be used as a linebacker and defensive back drill.
- Have the drill participants move back at a 45-degree angle after they have completed their four-up and two-back stepping.
- The drill can be conducted with any number of drill stations (when more than one drill station is used, a minimum distance of 25 yards should be maintained between drill stations).
- Vary the distances between the cones.

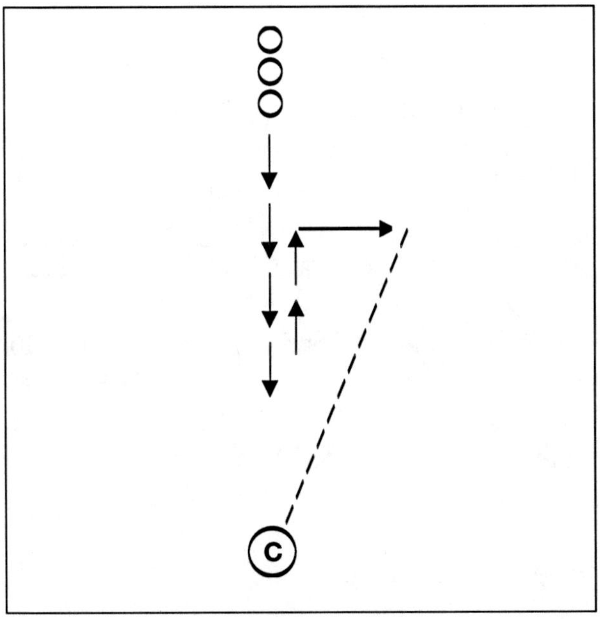

"T" Cone Drill

Keith James
Assistant Coach, Coastal Carolina University

Objective: To develop agility and speed. Incorporated are skills related to catching a thrown pass.

Equipment Needed: Four cones

Description:

- Place four cones (A, B, C, and D) in the shape of the letter T. A distance of 10 yards separates each cone (see the diagram).
- Align a row of tight ends behind and to the right of cone A.
- The coach, holding a football, is positioned adjacent to the row of tight ends.
- On the coach's command, the first tight end sprints to and then around cone B.
- The tight end lateral shuffles to and around cone C, and continues the shuffle to and around cone D.
- The tight end sprints back toward cone B and catches the football thrown by the coach.
- After catching the football, the tight end finishes the drill by turning and sprinting upfield for 10 yards.
- Drill continues until all tight ends have had a sufficient number of repetitions, moving both left and right around cone B.

Coaching Points:

- Always check to see that all tight ends are in their proper stances before starting the drill.
- Insist that the drill be conducted at full speed.
- Emphasize the importance of maintaining the proper body alignment throughout the drill.
- When sprinting from cone D to cone B, make sure that the tight end turns their heads and focus their eyes on the coach.
- Insist that the tight ends finish the drill by sprinting past cone A.

Safety Considerations:

- Proper warm-up should precede the drill.
- The drill area should be clear of all foreign articles.

Variation:

- Vary the distance between the cones.

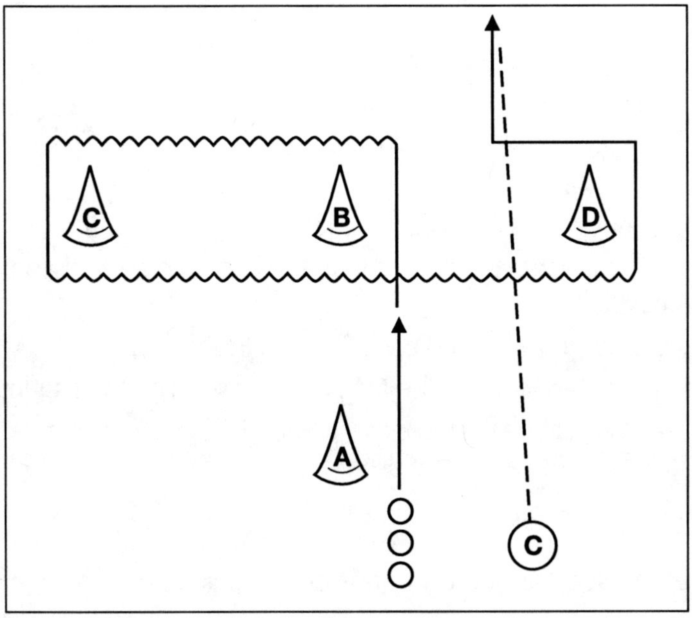

Cone Drill

Rocky Hager
Head Coach, Northeastern University

Objective: To develop agility and speed. Incorporated are skills related to running the stem route and catching a pass.

Equipment Needed: Five cones and footballs

Description:

- Place four cones (A, B, C, and D) seven yards apart to form a square. A fifth cone (E) is placed in the center of the square (see the diagram).
- Position a row of tight ends below and to the left of cone D.
- The coach, holding a football, is positioned below cone A.
- On the coach's cadence and snap count, the first tight end drives from his stance and sprints past cone C.
- The tight end stems back toward cone E and catches the pass thrown by the coach.
- After catching the thrown pass, the tight end turns upfield and sprints for 10 yards.
- The drill continues until all tight ends have had a sufficient number of repetitions from both a left- and right-square alignment.

Coaching Points:

- Always check to see that the tight ends are in their proper stances before starting the drill.
- Insist that the drill be conducted at full speed.
- Emphasize the importance of maintaining proper body alignment, with arms pumping throughout the drill.
- Insist that tight ends burst back toward cone E in running the stem route.
- In finishing the drill, instruct the defensive end to catch the football, tuck it away, and turn and sprint 10 yards upfield.

Safety Considerations:

- Proper warm-up should precede the drill.
- The drill area should be clear of all foreign articles.

Variations:

- Vary the distance between the cones.
- Have the tight end execute a variety of pass routes, using the different cones as a breaking point (dig/seam read, post/corner, and others).

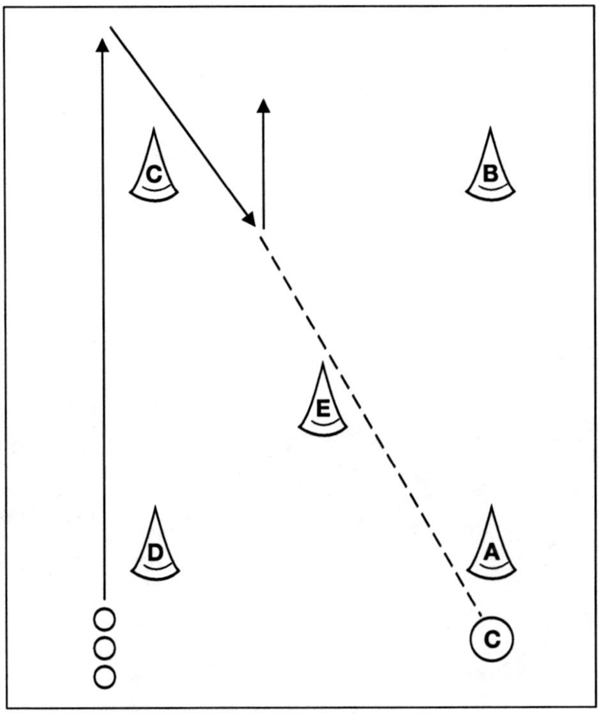

6

Defensive Back Drills

"N" Drill

Mike Sanford
Head Coach, University of Nevada, Las Vegas

Objective: To develop agility and speed. Incorporated are skill related to changing directions.

Equipment Needed: Four cones

Description:

- Align four cones (A, B, C, and D) five yards apart to for the letter N (see the diagram).
- Position defensive backs in a row adjacent to cone A.
- The coach is aligned at the midpoint of the two cones that form the top of the letter N.
- On the coach's command, the first defensive back drives from his three-point stance and sprints up and around cone B. The defensive back sprints back to and touches cone A.
- The defensive back backpedals diagonally to and touches cone C.
- The defensive back finishes the drill by sprinting past cone D.
- The drill continues until all defensive backs have had a sufficient number of repetitions, starting from both the left and right side of the letter N.

Coaching Points:

- Always check to see that the defensive backs are in the proper three-point stances before starting the drill.
- Insist that the drill be conducted at full speed.
- Make sure all defensive backs maintain the proper body alignment as they run and backpedal around and through the cones.
- Insist that all defensive backs sprint full speed past the last cone.

Safety Considerations:

- Proper warm-up should precede the drill.
- The drill area should be clear of all foreign articles.

Variations:

- The drill can be used as a general agility and speed drill for all skill positions.
- Set up two different drill stations and have completion between defensive backs.

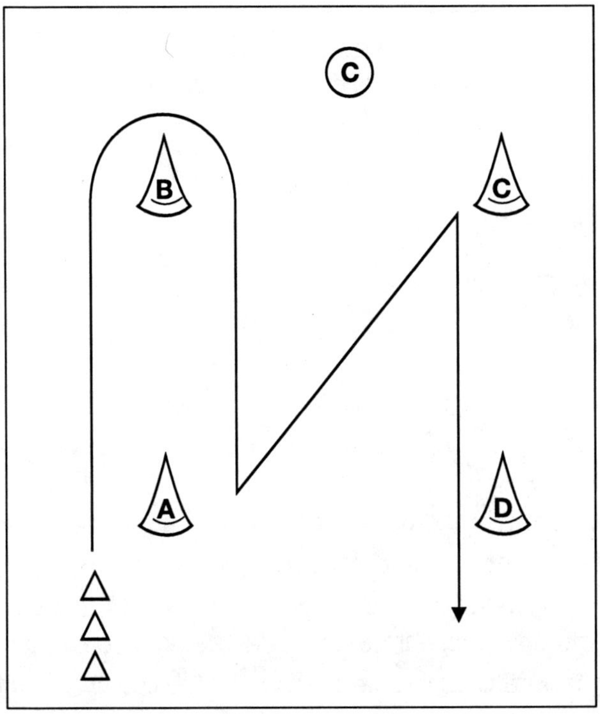
C
B
C
A
D

Backpedal Transition Drill

Leslie Frazier
Assistant Coach, Minnesota Vikings

Objective: To develop agility and speed. Incorporated are skills related to breaking on and intercepting a pass.

Equipment Needed: Footballs

Description:

- Position a defensive back on a selected line of scrimmage.
- The coach, holding a football, stands five yards in front of and facing the defensive back.
- Other defensive backs stand adjacent to the drill area.
- On the coach's command, the defensive back backpedals for 10 yards.
- On the coach's signal, turning the shoulders left or right, the defensive back plants his back foot and drives forward at a 45-degree angle back toward the coach.
- The defensive back catches the pass thrown by the coach, tucks it away, and sprints upfield.
- The drill continues until all defensive backs have had a sufficient number of repetitions, cutting at a 45-degree angle both to the left and to the right.

Coaching Points:

- Always check to see that the running backs are in their proper stances before starting the drill.
- Insist that the drill be conducted at full speed.
- Make sure that all defensive backs maintain the proper body alignment throughout the drill.
- Insist that the defensive back sprints upfield after catching the thrown pass.
- Instruct the defensive backs to keep their heads up and their eyes focused on the coach at all times.

Safety Considerations:

- Proper warm-up should precede the drill.
- The drill area should be clear of all foreign articles.
- To avoid falling, instruct all defensive backs to the proper mechanics for the execution of the backpedal.

Variations:

- The drill can be used as a linebacker drill.
- Have more than one defensive back participating at a time, with the coach throwing the football to any of the defensive backs.

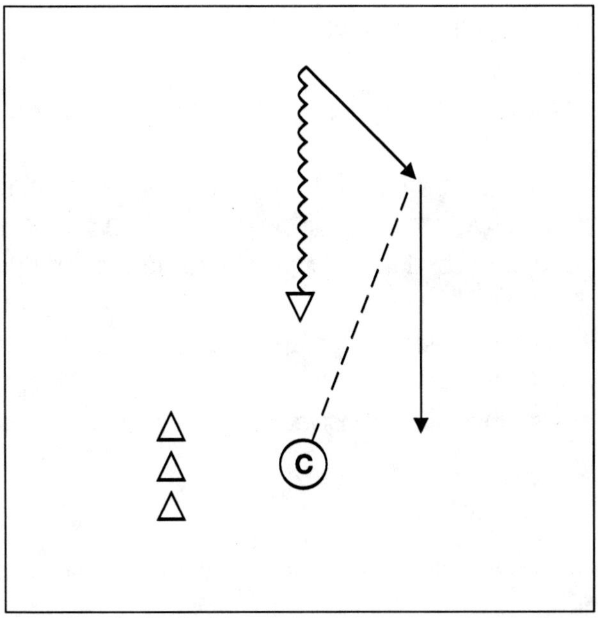

Zigzag Drills

Sylvester Croon
Head Coach, Mississippi State University

Objective: To develop agility and speed. Incorporated are skills related to reading the quarterback, changing directions, and intercepting a pass.

Equipment Needed: Footballs

Description:

- Align four defensive backs five yards apart in a selected yard line.
- Other defensive backs stand adjacent to the drill man.
- Position a coach (quarterback), holding a football, five yards in front of and facing the defensive backs.
- On the coach's command, showing pass, the four defensive backs begin their backpedals.
- On the coach's second command, turning the shoulder either left or right, the defensive backs will drive back at a 45-degree angle in the designated direction.
- After three shoulder turns and the change of directions by the defensive backs, the coach passes the football.
- One of the four defensive backs intercepts the thrown pass, and all four defensive backs sprint upfield and past the coach.
- The drill continues until all defensive backs have had a sufficient number of repetitions.

Coaching Points:

- Always check to see that the defensive backs are in their proper stances before starting the drill.
- Instruct the defensive backs to read and react to the coach's shoulder turns.
- Emphasize the importance of always intercepting the pass at its highest point.
- After the interception is made, insist that all defensive backs sprint back upfield past the coach.

Safety Considerations:

- Proper warm-up should precede the drill.
- The drill area should be clear of all foreign articles.
- It is recommended that the drill be conducted at three-quarter speed.

Variation:

- The drill can be used as a linebacker drill.

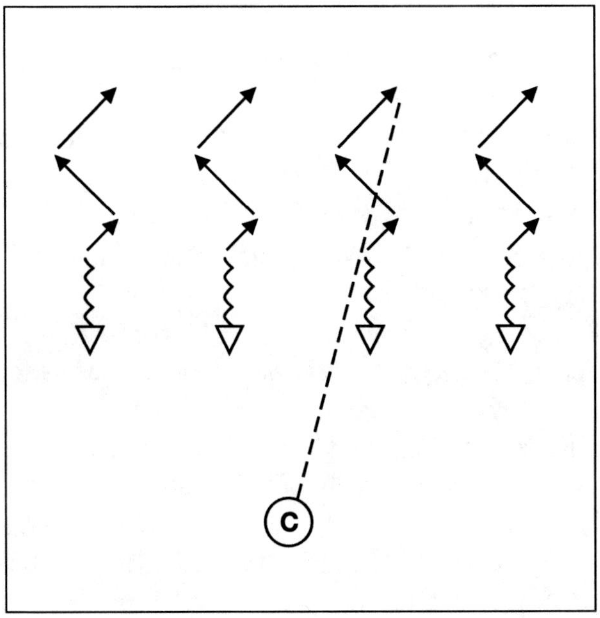

Break Drill

Zak Willis
Head Coach, Newberry College

Objective: To develop agility and speed. Incorporated are skills related to intercepting a pass.

Equipment Needed: Footballs

Description:

- Align two wide receivers (or defensive backs) 12 yards apart on the opponent's 15-yard line.
- Position a defensive back five yards in front of and at the midpoint of the two receivers (see the diagram).
- Other defensive backs stand adjacent to the drill man.
- The coach (quarterback), holding football, is positioned in the standard quarterback/receiver alignment.
- On the coach's cadence and ball snap, the defensive back will backpedal into the zone at the midpoint between the two wide receivers, while focusing his eyes on the coach.
- As the coach turn his shoulders to deliver the pass to either of the wide receivers, the defensive back reads the coach's motion and breaks to and intercepts the thrown pass.
- After interception is made, the defensive back tucks the football away and sprints down the near sideline for the score.
- The drill continues until all defensive backs have had a sufficient number of repetitions from both a left and right quarterback-receiver alignment.

Coaching Points:

- Always check to see that the defensive backs are in their proper stances before starting the drill.
- Insist that the drill be conducted at full speed.
- Instruct defensive backs as to the proper mechanics in the execution of the backpedal.
- Emphasize the importance of always keeping the head up with eyes focused on the coach throughout the drill.
- Insist that the defensive backs intercept the football at its highest point and sprint full speed down the sideline after the interception is made.

Safety Considerations:

- Proper warm-up should precede the drill.
- The drill area should be clear of all foreign articles.
- Instruct the wide receivers that they are not to contest the defensive backs for the football, but allow them to intercept the pass unimpeded.

Variation:

- The drill can be used as a linebacker drill by changing the wide-receivers-quarterback-alignment relationship.

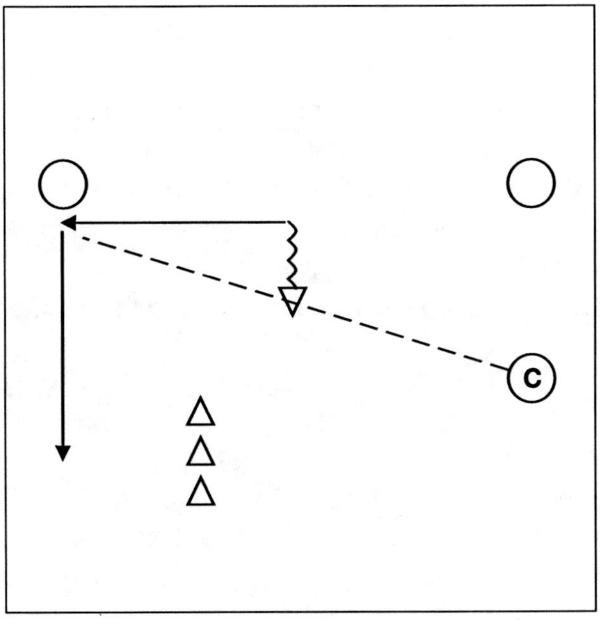

Change-of-Direction Lateral Breaks Drill

Rocky Long
Head Coach, University of New Mexico

Objective: To develop agility and speed. Incorporated are skills related to intercepting a pass.

Equipment Needed: Footballs

Description:

- Position a defensive back at the midpoint of a selected yard line.
- Other defensive backs stand adjacent to the drill area.
- The coach (passer), holding a football, is aligned 12 yards to the left and 10 yards behind, and in a front-facing alignment to the defensive back (see the diagram).
- On the coach's command, the first defensive back backpedals for five yards, plants the back foot, and sprints at a 45-degree angle to his right for five yards.
- The defensive back turns and sprints laterally to his right at a 90-degree angle for another five yards.
- Next, the defensive back opens his hips and executes another backpedal for 10 yards.
- When finishing the drill, the defensive back again sprints laterally at a 90-degree angle for five yards, intercepts the pass thrown by the coach, and sprints five yards downfield.
- The drill continues until all defensive backs have had a sufficient number of repetitions, moving from both a left and right drill alignment.

Coaching Points:

- Always check to make sure that the defensive backs are in their proper stances before starting the drill.
- Insist that the drill be conducted at full speed.
- Make sure that all defensive backs maintain the proper body alignment, with their eyes focused on the coach throughout the drill.
- Insist that all defensive backs sprint five yards downfield after the interception is made.

Safety Considerations:

- Proper warm-up should precede the drill.
- The drill area should be clear of all foreign articles.

Variation:

- Replace the last 90-degree-angle break with a turn-and-run deep cut.

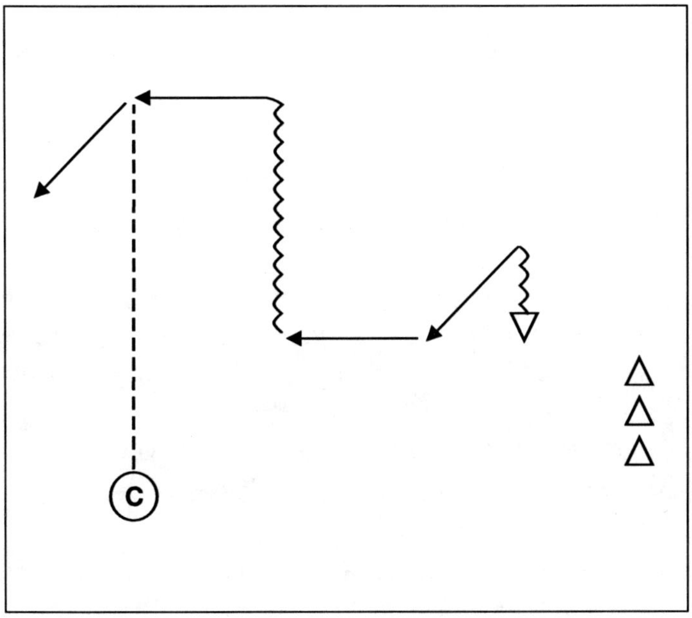

Touch-and-Turn Drill

Sonny Lubick
Head Coach, Colorado State University

Objective: To develop agility and speed. Incorporated are skills related to changing directions.

Equipment Needed: Footballs

Description:

- Position four cones (A, B, C, and D) 10 yards apart to form a square (see the diagram).
- Align a row of defensive backs adjacent to cone A.
- The coach is positioned at the midpoint and five yards below the base of the square.
- On the coach's command, the first defensive back drives from his stance and sprints diagonally to cone C. After touching cone C with his right hand, the defensive back turns and sprints to cone D, which he again touches with his right hand.
- The defensive back turns left and sprints diagonally to cone B.
- After touching cone B with the right hand, the defensive back turns left and finishes the drill by sprinting five yards past cone A.
- The drill continues until all defensive backs have had a sufficient number of repetitions, starting from both the left and right side of the square (when beginning the drill from the right side of the square, hand touches are with the left hand and turns are to the right).

Coaching Points:

- Always check to see that the defensive backs are in proper stances before starting the drill.
- Insist that the drill be conducted at full speed.
- Instruct the defensive backs to stay tight to the cone line and when coming out of the turn to sprint in a straight line to the next cone.
- Insist that all defensive backs finish the drill by sprinting five yards past cone A.

Safety Considerations:

- Proper warm-up should precede the drill.
- The drill area should be clear of all foreign articles.
- Alert defensive backs who are waiting to perform the drill to stay clear of the drill-finish area.

Variations:

- The drill can be used as an agility and speed drill for all positions.
- Vary the distances be the cones.

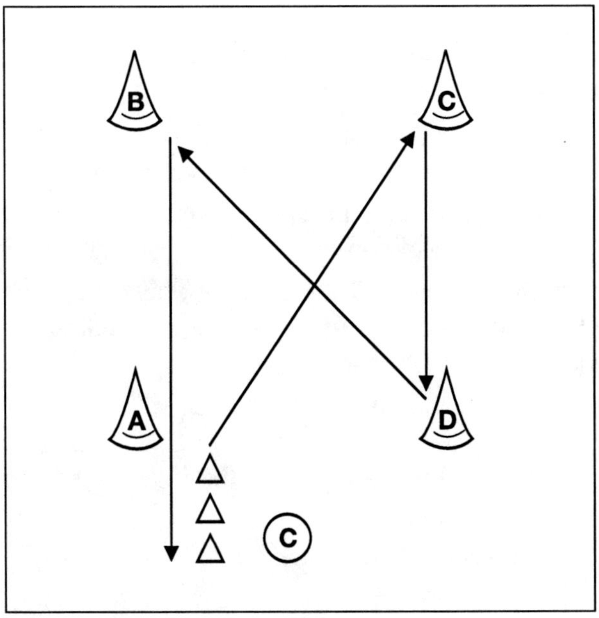

Ladder Whip Drill

Ed Orgeron
Head Coach, University of Mississippi

Objective: To develop agility and speed. Incorporated are skills related to the proper execution of the backpedal and intercepting a pass.

Equipment Needed: Footballs

Description:

- Align a defensive back on a selected yard line. Other defensive backs stand adjacent to the drill area (see the diagram).
- The coach (passer), holding a football, is positioned in a front-facing alignment and five yards from the defensive back.
- On the coach's movement, pulling the football to his chest and turning his shoulders, the first defensive back initiates his backpedal
- The defensive back continues his backpedal until the coach raises the football to the pass ready position. The defensive back turns and sprints downfield.
- After the defensive back sprints 5 to 10 yards downfield, the coach exaggerates either a turn-left or -right shoulder movement, and the defensive back sprints at a 45-degree angle in that direction for three to five yards.
- When finishing the drill, the coach raises his downfield shoulder (simulating the preparation for a long pass), and the defensive back immediately changes direction, sprints downfield while whipping the head around, and locates, sprints to, and intercepts the pass thrown by the coach.
- After intercepting the pass, the defensive back turns and sprints back upfield.
- The drill continues until all defensive backs have had a sufficient number of repetitions.

Coaching Points:

- Always check to see that the defensive backs are in their proper stances before starting the drill.
- Insist that the drill be conducted at full speed.
- Make sure defensive backs maintain the proper body alignment throughout the drill.
- Instruct all defensive backs to maintain eye contact with the coach at all times.

- Stress the importance of whipping the head around to locate the football, when sprinting to intercept the pass.
- After the pass is intercepted, insist that all defensive backs secure the football and sprint back past the coach.

Safety Considerations:

- Proper warm-up should precede the drill.
- The drill area should be clear of all foreign articles.

Variation:

- The football can be thrown at different times during the drill.

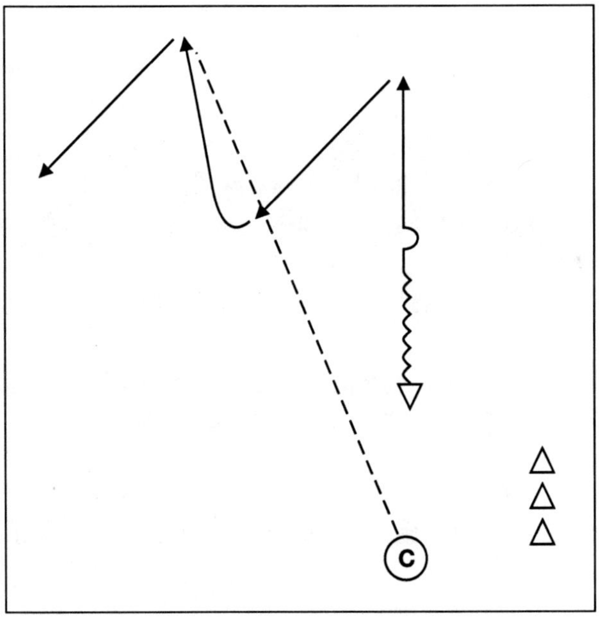

Stretcher Drill

Tom O'Brien
Head Coach, North Carolina State University

Objective: To develop agility and speed. Incorporated are skills related to intercepting a pass.

Equipment Needed: Footballs

Description:

- Align two defensive backs 10 yards apart on a selected yard line. Designate one as a pass receiver and the other as the defensive back (see the diagram).
- Other defensive backs and designated wide receivers stand adjacent to the drill area.
- Position the coach (passer) in a front-facing alignment midway between and 10 yards upfield from the defensive back and wide receiver.
- On the coach's command, the defensive back begins his backpedal, and the receiver runs a pass pattern straight down the field.
- At some point during the backpedal, the coach turns his shoulders and throws a pass to the receiver.
- The defensive back reads and reacts to the coach's shoulder turn, and sprints to and intercepts the pass.
- The drill continues until all defensive backs have had a sufficient number of repetitions, both from a left and right drill alignment.

Coaching Points:

- Always check to see that all defensive backs are in their proper stance before starting the drill
- Insist that the drill be conducted at full speed.
- Instruct the defensive backs to always keep their eyes on the passer and to read and react quickly on the coach's shoulder turn.
- Make sure the defensive backs intercept the pass at its highest point and sprint upfield 10 yards after the interception is made.

Safety Considerations:

- Proper warm-up should precede the drill.
- The drill area should be clear of all foreign articles.
- Instruct the receivers that they are not to contest the defensive backs for the football, but to allow them to intercept the football unimpeded.

Variations:

- Position the defensive back and receiver wider apart and farther downfield from the coach.
- Increase the velocity and trajectory of the thrown pass.

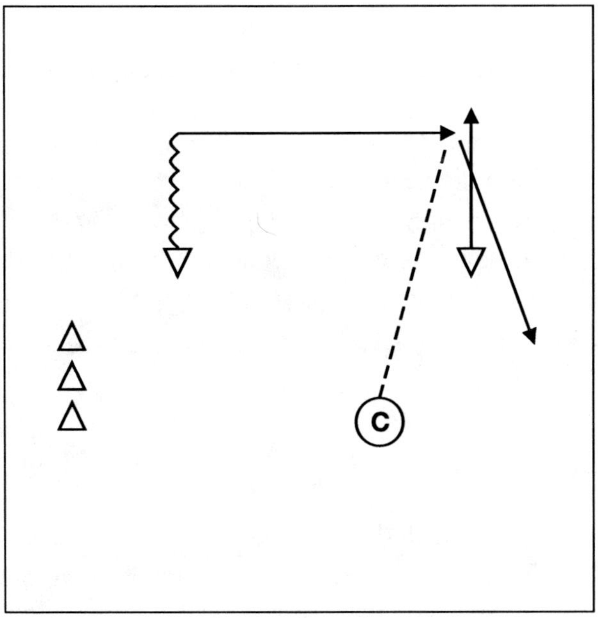

Five-Yard Weave Drill

Danny Rocco
Head Coach, Liberty University

Objective: To develop agility and speed. Incorporated are skills related to the proper execution of the backpedal weave.

Equipment Needed: Footballs

Description:

- Position a defensive back in a football ready position on the intersection of a selected yard line and a sideline. The defensive back faces the sideline (see the diagram).
- Other defensive backs stand adjacent to the drill area.
- The coach is positioned in a front-facing alignment and five yards in front of the defensive back.
- On the coach's command ("Set, hut"), the first defensive back backpedals at a 45-degree angle in the direction signaled by the coach.
- At a designated point in the backpedal, the coach will direct the defensive back to change directions and execute the backpedal in the opposite direction.
- The previous two descriptions are repeated four or five times.
- The drill continues until all defensive backs have had a sufficient number of repetitions.

Coaching Points:

- Always check to see that the defensive backs are in their proper stances before starting the drill.
- Insist that the drill be conducted at full speed.
- Instruct the defensive backs to work for a depth of six or seven yards as they execute the backpedal weave, both left and right.
- Emphasize the importance of maintaining eye contact with the coach throughout the drill.
- Insist that the defensive backs maintain the proper backpedal-weave body alignment throughout the drill.

Safety Considerations:

- Proper warm-up should precede the drill.
- The drill area should be clear of all foreign articles.

Variations:

- Incorporate a thrown pass and have the defensive backs intercept the pass.
- The drill can be used as a linebacker drill.
- Have multiple defensive backs performing the drill at the same time (a distance of five yards should be maintained between the defensive backs).

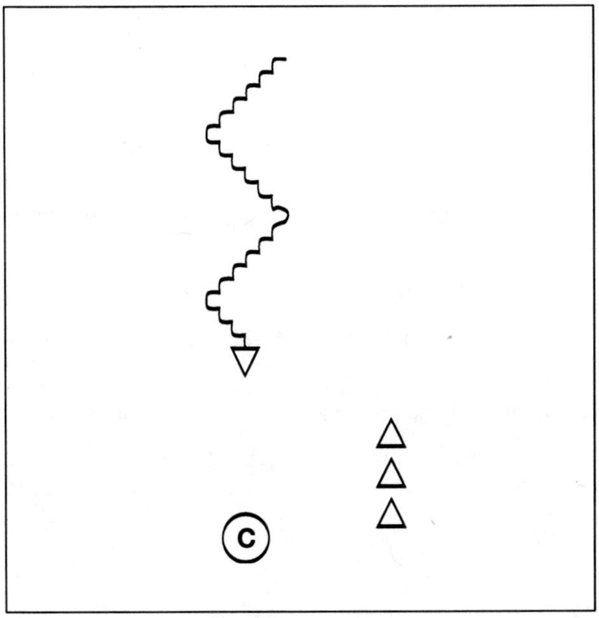

Four Corners Drill

Mike Kramer
Former Head Coach, Montana State University

Objective: To develop agility and speed. Incorporated are skills related to executing the backpedal, changing directions, and intercepting a pass.

Equipment Needed: Four cones and footballs

Description:

- Align four cones (A, B, C, and D) seven yards apart to form a square (see the diagram).
- Position a defensive back, in the football ready position, in front of and facing cone A.
- Other defensive backs stand adjacent to the drill area.
- The coach, holding a football, is positioned at the midpoint and 10 yards below the base of the square.
- On the coach's command, the first defensive back backpedals to cone B.
- When the defensive back reaches cone B, he plants his back foot and sprints diagonally to cone D.
- When reaching cone D, the defensive back again backpedals to cone C, plants his back foot, and sprints diagonally to cone A as the coach passes the defensive back the football.
- On the coach's second command, the second defensive back begins his backpedal to cone B once the first defensive back has reached the three-quarter mark of his first diagonal sprint to cone D. When executed in this manner, the first defensive back will catch the thrown pass by the coach just after the second defensive back crosses the midpoint (see the X on the diagram) of his diagonal sprint from cone B to cone D.
- The drill continues until all defensive backs have had a sufficient number of repetitions, starting from both the left and right sides of the square.

Coaching Points:

- Always check to see that the defensive backs are in the football ready position before starting the drill.
- Insist that the drill be conducted at full speed.
- Make sure all defensive backs execute the backpedal correctly.

Safety Considerations:

- Proper warm-up should precede the drill.
- The drill area should be clear of all foreign articles.
- The coach should monitor closely the point of the drill at which the two players intersect each other.
- Alert the defensive backs who are waiting to perform the drill to stay clear of drill-finish area.

Variations:

- Vary the distances between the cones.
- The drill can be used as a linebacker drill.

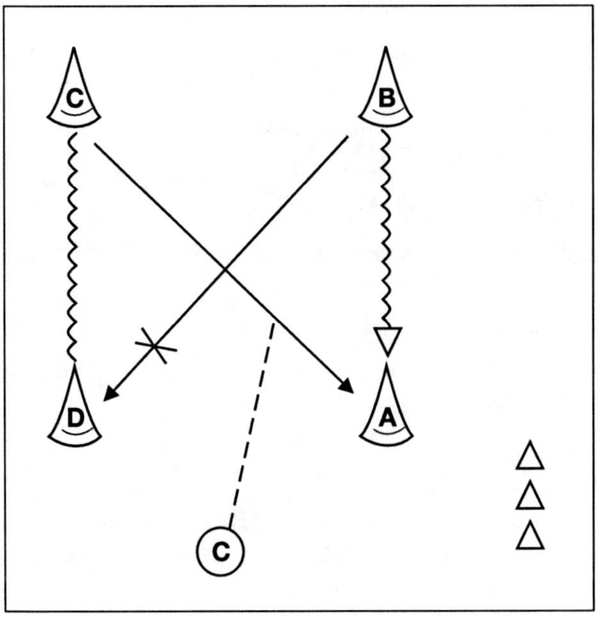

Box Shuffle Drill

Larry Kehres
Head Coach, Mount Union College

Objective: To develop agility and speed. Incorporated are skills related to executing the backpedal and intercepting a pass.

Equipment Needed: Four cones, three half-moon agility bags, and footballs

Description:

- Align four cones (A, B, C, and D) seven yards apart to form a square. Place three agility bags three yards behind and parallel to the cone A. Two yards separate the three bags (see the diagram).
- Position a defensive back in the football ready position adjacent to the cone and facing the three bags.
- Other defensive backs stand adjacent to the drill area.
- The coach, holding a football, is positioned two yards behind cone C.
- On the coach's command, the first defensive back backpedals diagonally to cone B, plants his back foot, and sprints to cone C.
- At cone C, the defensive back comes under control and backpedals diagonally to cone D.
- At cone D, the defensive back again plants his back foot and sprints to cone A and the three-bag area. The defensive back comes under control, turns and faces the coach, and shuffles over the three bags.
- In finishing the drill, the defensive back sprints toward and intercepts the pass thrown by the coach.
- The drill continues until all defensive backs have had a sufficient number of repetitions, starting from both the left and right side of the square.

Coaching Points:

- Always check to see that the defensive backs are in the football ready position before starting the drill.
- Insist that the drill be conducted at full speed.
- Instruct the defensive backs to maintain the proper body alignment as they execute the backpedals and sprint from one cone to the other.

- Emphasize the importance of always keeping the head up and eyes focused straight ahead.
- Instruct the defensive backs in catching the pass to always catch it at its highest point.

Safety Considerations:

- Proper warm-up should precede the drill.
- The drill area should be clear of all foreign articles.

Variations:

- Have the defensive backs backpedal and weave instead of just having them backpedal.
- Substitute the pass catch with a scoop-and-score.
- The drill can be used as a competitive drill by recording the times it takes for the defensive backs to move through the drill.

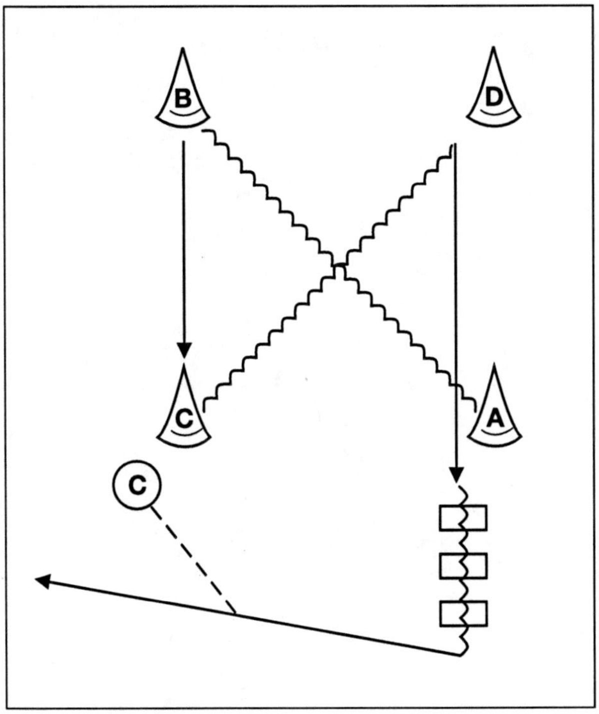

7

Defensive Line Drills

Edge Pass-Rush Drill

Mel Tjeerdsma
Head Coach, Northwest Missouri State University

Objective: To develop agility and speed. Incorporated are skills related to rushing the passer.

Equipment Needed: Two cones

Description:

- Align a cone on a selected yard line to represent the offensive guard or tackle position. A second cone is placed four yards behind the first cone.
- Position a row of defensive linemen just to the outside of the front cone.
- Position a quarterback (manager), holding a football, at the center position.
- The coach stands adjacent to the drill area.
- On the quarterback's cadence and simulated ball snap, the first defensive lineman drives from his stance as the quarterback drops to his designated pass-drop position.
- When the defensive lineman reaches the second cone, he plants his outside foot and accelerates through the quarterback.
- The drill continues until all defensive linemen have had a sufficient number of repetitions, starting from both a left and a right defensive alignment.

Coaching Points:

- Always check to see that the defensive linemen are aligned correctly and are in their proper stances before starting the drill.
- Insist that the drill be conducted at full speed.
- Instruct the offensive linemen to lower their hips, and to step flat with the inside foot as they round the second cone.
- Emphasize the importance of always turning the edge off the plant of the outside foot.

Safety Considerations:

- Proper warm-up should precede the drill.
- The drill area should be clear of all foreign articles.
- Defensive linemen with lower-body injuries should be excused from this drill.

Variations:

- The drill can be used as a general agility drill for all pass-rush positions.
- Set up multiple drill stations. Make sure all defensive linemen are executing the pass rush in the same direction.
- Incorporate blockers instead of cones.

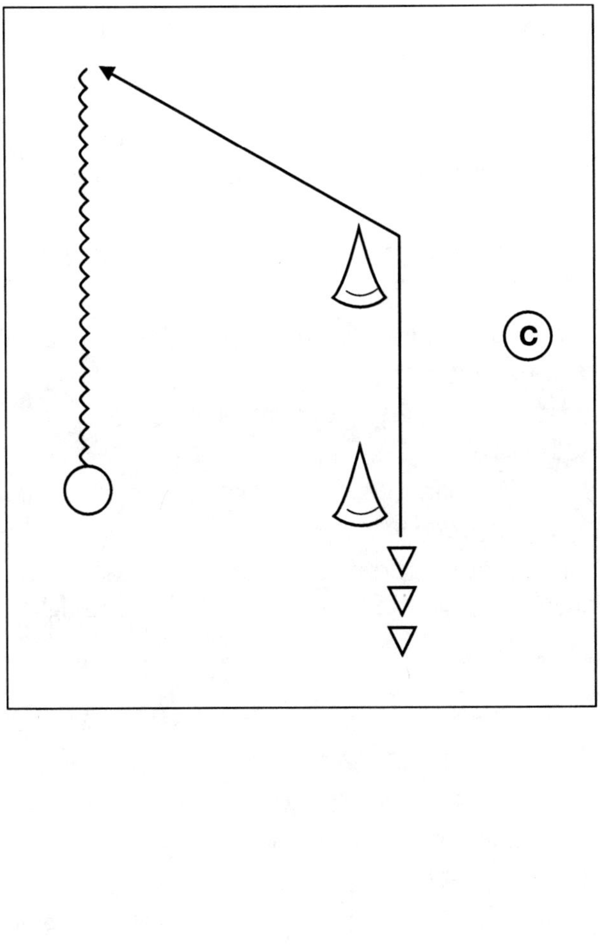

Triangle Drill

Chuck Broyles
Head Coach, Pittsburg State University

Objective: To develop agility and speed. Incorporated are skills related to changing directions and acceleration.

Equipment Needed: Four rectangular bags and a cone

Description:

- Align four rectangular bags perpendicular to a selected yard line. Two yards separate each bag. Place a cone at the midpoint and three yards in front of the bags (see the diagram).
- Position a row of offensive linemen at one end of the row of bags.
- The coach stands behind the cone.
- The first offensive lineman drives from his three-point stance and sprints through the four bags, placing one foot between each bag.
- After sprinting past the bags, the offensive lineman plants his backside foot, turns, and sprints past the cone.
- As the first offensive lineman runs over the last bag, the second lineman will begin his run, and the pattern continues.
- The drill continues until all offensive linemen have had a sufficient number of repetitions, sprinting through the bags from both left and right.

Coaching Points:

- Always check to see that the defensive linemen are in their proper stances before starting the drill.
- Insist the drill be conducted at full speed.
- Instruct the defensive linemen to drop their hips, plant the outside foot, turn, and sprint in a straight line past the cone.
- Insist that the defensive linemen sprint past the cone in finishing the drill.

Safety Considerations:

- Proper warm-up should precede the drill.
- The drill area should be clear of all foreign articles.

Variations:

- The drill can be used as a general agility and speed drill for all positions.
- Add additional bags.
- Vary the distance between the bags.
- Have the coach drop a football as the defensive lineman passes the cone for a scoop-and-score.

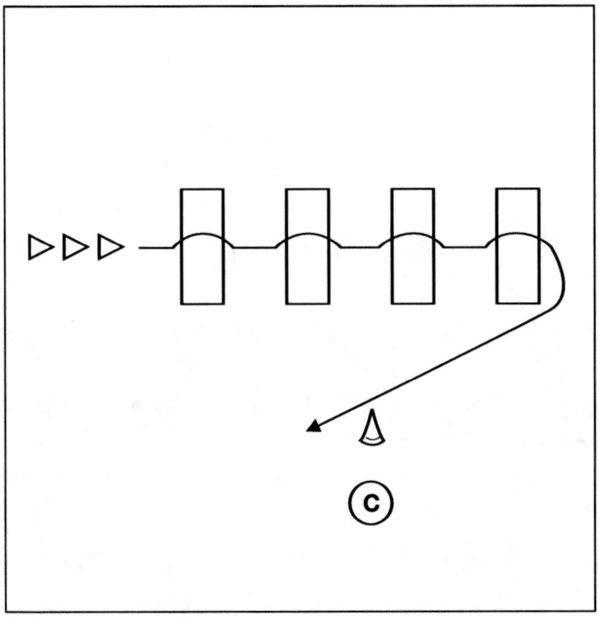

Figure Eight Drill

Dave Clawson
Head Coach, University of Richmond

Objective: To develop agility and speed. Incorporated are skills related to rushing the passer.

Equipment Needed: Two hoops (12 feet in diameter), an arm pad (for the coach), and a football

Description:

- Place two hoops, one on top of the other, adjacent to a selected yard line. One yard separates the two hoops. Place two cones 13 feet apart and three yards in front of the lower hoop (see the diagram).
- A center (manager), holding a football, is positioned just inside the bottom of the lower hoop.
- Align a row of defensive linemen adjacent to the cone on the left side of the lower hoop.
- A coach, with a protective arm pad on his outside arm, is positioned on the left, inside the edge of the first hoop.
- On the manager's cadence and ball snap, the first defensive lineman drives from his stance and runs a figure-eight pattern around the two hoops (see the diagram).
- As the defensive lineman passes the coach, the defensive lineman knocks down the near arm of the coach with a chop to the outside arm pad, while executing a rip technique around the coach.
- The coach moves to the inside edge on the opposite side of the lower hoop and awaits the return of the defensive lineman, where the previous description is repeated.
- The defensive lineman finishes the drill by sprinting past the cone at the bottom right of the lower hoop.
- The drill continues until all defensive linemen have had a sufficient number of repetitions, starting from both the left and right cones.

Coaching Points:

- Always check to see that the defensive linemen are in their proper stances before starting the drill.
- Insist that the drill be conducted at full speed.
- Instruct the defensive linemen to lean inside as they run around the two hoops.

- Instruct the defensive linemen to the proper mechanics in the execution of the chop and rip techniques.
- Instruct the defensive linemen to run around the hoops with their arms pumping (no skipping).
- Insist that the defensive linemen finish the drill by sprinting past the front cone.

Safety Considerations:

- Proper warm-up should precede the drill.
- The drill area should be clear of all foreign articles.
- The drill should not be conducted when the ground is slippery.

Variations:

- Vary the distance between the bags.
- The drill can be used with a single hoop and place a pop-up bag to designate a quarterback.

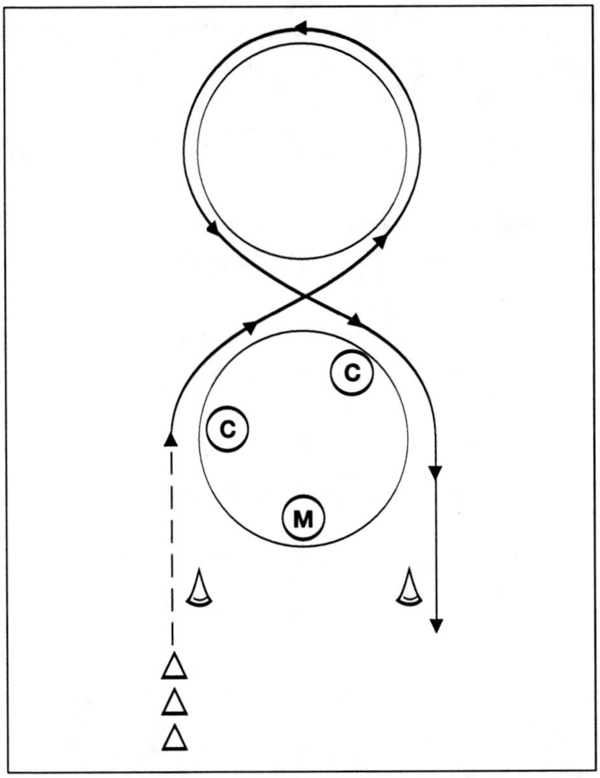

Progressive Shuffle Drill

Jeff Hafley
Assistant Coach, University of Pittsburgh

Objective: To develop agility and speed. Incorporated are skills related to changing directions.

Equipment Needed: Eight cones

Description:

- Align two rows of cones with four cones in each row. Fifteen yards separate the two rows of cones, and five yards separate the cones in each row. The first cone in each row is placed on a selected yard line (see the diagram).
- Position three defensive linemen, in their stances and equal distances apart, on a selected yard line.
- Other defensive linemen stand adjacent to the drill area.
- The coach, holding a football, is positioned in front of the first three linemen.
- On the coach's cadence and ball snap, the three defensive linemen drive from their stances, sprint to the next yard line five yards upfield, and touch that line with the right hand.
- The linemen redirect, sprint back to the starting line, and touch that line with the left hand.
- The previous two descriptions are repeated by sprinting 10 yards up and back, and then sprinting 15 yards up and back, touching each yard line with the designated hand.
- The drill continues until all defensive linemen have had a sufficient number of repetitions.

Coaching Points:

- Always check to see that the defensive linemen are in their proper stances before starting the drill.
- Insist that the drill be conducted at full speed.
- Insist that all defensive linemen touch every yard line with the designated hand.
- Instruct the defensive linemen not to round off their turns and not to take false steps.
- Emphasize the importance of always keeping the head up with eyes focused straight ahead.

Safety Considerations:

- Proper warm-up should precede the drill.
- The drill area should be clear of all foreign articles.
- Alert defensive linemen who are waiting to perform the drill to stay clear of the drill-finish area.
- Instruct defensive linemen to always touch the upfield yard lines with the right hand and the downfield yard lines with the left hand (this technique decreases the chance of a collision occurring).

Variations:

- The drill can be used as a general agility and speed drill for all positions.
- Use a variety of ways of moving to the yard lines (shuffle, backward run, carioca, etc.).
- Change the sequence of touching the upfield lines (such as 15-10-5, 10-5-15, or 5-10-15).
- Place three footballs just past the ending point of the drill and execute a scoop-and-score opportunity.
- Make the drill competitive by timing the different defensive linemen.

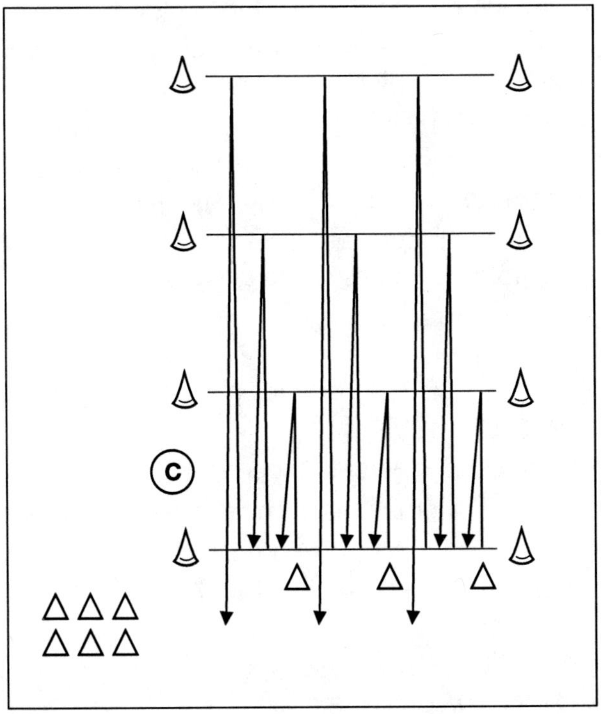

Change-of-Direction Big Bag Drill

Derrick Jackson
Assistant Coach, Syracuse University

Objective: To develop agility and speed. Incorporated are skills related to reacting and changing directions.

Equipment Needed: Five agility bags, two cones, and footballs

Description:

- Align five agility bags one yard apart and perpendicular to a selected yard line. Place two cones one yard beyond and three yards outside of the row of bags (see the diagram).
- Position a row of defensive linemen adjacent to and facing sideways to the first bag.
- A coach stands across from the row of linemen, and a second coach is positioned at the far end of the bags.
- On the first coach's command, the first defensive lineman assumes the football ready position beside the first bag and then works laterally through the bags, stepping both feet in each space between the bags.
- On the first coach's whistle, the defensive lineman changes the direction of his lateral stepping and moves back past the first bag.
- On the first coach's second whistle, the defensive lineman turns and sprints over the last bag at the end of the drill area as the second coach gives a hand signal for the defensive lineman to sprint either left or right past the cone on that side.
- The drill continues until all defensive linemen have had a sufficient number of repetitions, starting from both ends of the bags.

Coaching Points:

- Always check to see that the defensive linemen are in the football ready position before starting the drill.
- Insist that the drill be conducted at full speed.
- Make sure the defensive linemen maintain the desired body alignment throughout the drill.
- Insist that the defensive linemen finish the drill by sprinting past the designated cone.

Safety Considerations:

- Proper warm-up should precede the drill.
- The drill area should be clear of all foreign articles.

Variations:

- The drill can be used as a general agility and speed drill for all positions.
- Vary the number of bags and the distance between the bags.
- Replace the cones with pop-up dummies and have defensive linemen finish with a pass rush move.

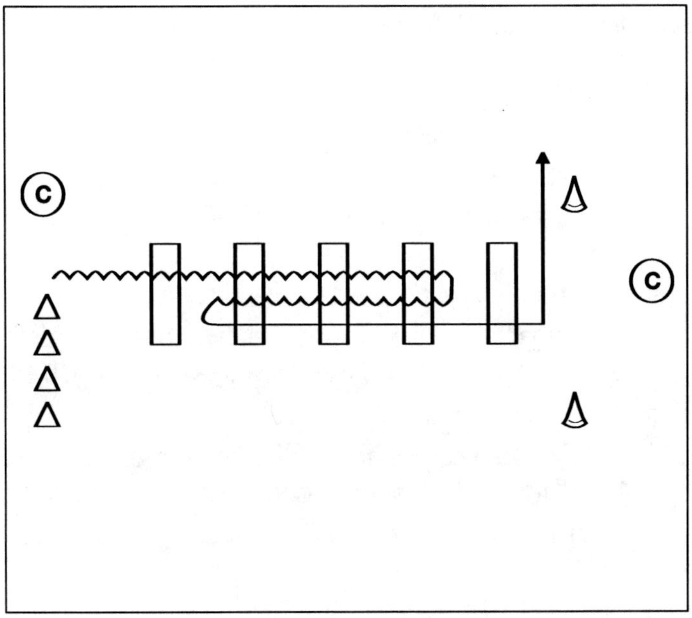

Hoop Figure Eight Drill

Richard Wright
Assistant Coach, Northwest Missouri State University

Objective: To develop agility and speed. Incorporated are skills related to rushing the passer.

Equipment Needed: Two hoops (12 feet in diameter) and a football on a stick

Description:

- Place two hoops, one on top of the other, adjacent to a selected yard line. Three yards separate the two hoops (see the diagram).
- Position a defensive lineman in a three-point stance, to the left of the rear-side base of the top circle.
- Other defensive linemen stand adjacent to the drill area.
- The coach, with a football on a stick, stands adjacent to the first defensive lineman.
- On the coach's cadence and ball snap, the first lineman explodes from his stance and circles around the top hoop.
- When the defensive lineman comes around the last turn of the top hoop, he quickly transitions his sprint around the bottom hoop, going in the opposite direction.
- The defensive lineman finishes the drill by sprinting past the coach who is positioned between the two hoops.
- The drill continues until all defensive linemen have had a sufficient number of repetitions.

Coaching Points:

- Always check to see that the defensive linemen are in their proper stances before starting the drill.
- Insist that the drill be conducted at full speed.
- Instruct defensive linemen to maintain a low center of gravity and to lean tight inside as they circle around the hoops.
- Insist that the defensive linemen finish the drill by sprinting past the coach.

Safety Considerations:

- Proper warm-up should precede the drill.
- The drill area should be clear of all foreign articles.
- The drill should not be conducted when the ground is slippery.

Variations:

- The drill can be used as an agility and speed drill for all pass-rush positions.
- Start a second defensive lineman at a designated distance behind the first defensive end to create a chase situation.
- Position shield holders at various points inside the hoops, and have them impede the progress of the defensive linemen as they circle the hoops.

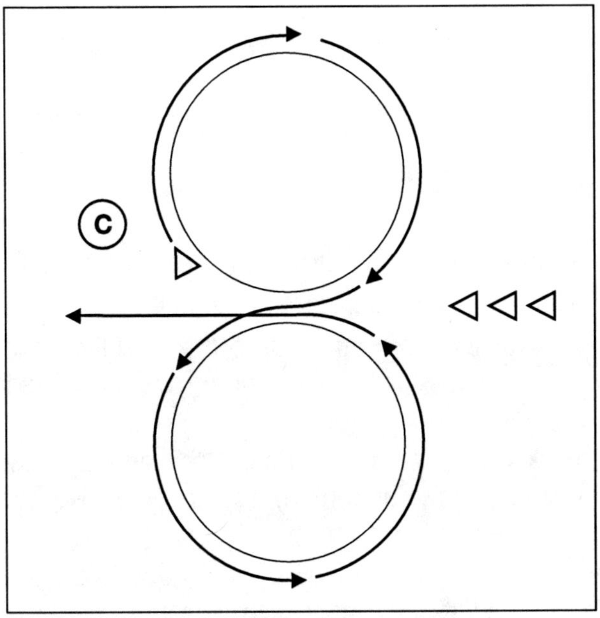

Speed Pass-Rush Drill

Joe Paterno
Head Coach, Pennsylvania State University

Objective: To develop agility and speed. Incorporated are skills related to rushing the passer, and reading and reacting to the draw and the outside-screen plays.

Equipment Needed: Footballs

Description:

- Position a center and two offensive linemen in their standard alignment on a selected yard line.
- A quarterback is positioned in a shotgun alignment five yards behind the center (see the diagram).
- Align a defensive lineman on the outside edge of each offensive lineman.
- Other defensive linemen stand adjacent to the drill area.
- The coach stands five yards in front of the center and flashes a finger signal—one finger for a pass, two fingers for a draw, three fingers for a screen—to the offensive linemen (see the diagrams).
- On the quarterback's cadence and ball snap, the offensive linemen execute the designated play (pass, draw, or screen) as the defensive linemen execute the appropriate pass rush, or read and react to the draw or screen.
- The drill continues until all defensive linemen have had a sufficient number of repetitions from both a left and a right alignment.

Coaching Points:

- Always check to see that the defensive linemen are aligned correctly and in their proper stances before starting the drill.
- Insist that the drill be conducted at full speed.
- Instruct defensive linemen to the proper methods of reading and reacting to the pass, screen, or draw.

Safety Considerations:

- Proper warm-up should precede the drill.
- The drill area should be clear of all foreign articles.
- Full equipment should be worn.
- The drill should progress from half speed to full speed.

- The coach should closely monitor the intensity of the drill.
- The coach should watch for and eliminate all unacceptable match-ups as to size and athletic ability.

Variations:

- Have the defensive linemen line up on either the outside or inside edge of the offensive linemen.
- Vary the alignment of the offensive linemen.
- The drill can be used as a pass-protection drill for the offensive linemen.
- Start the drill with the quarterback under the center.

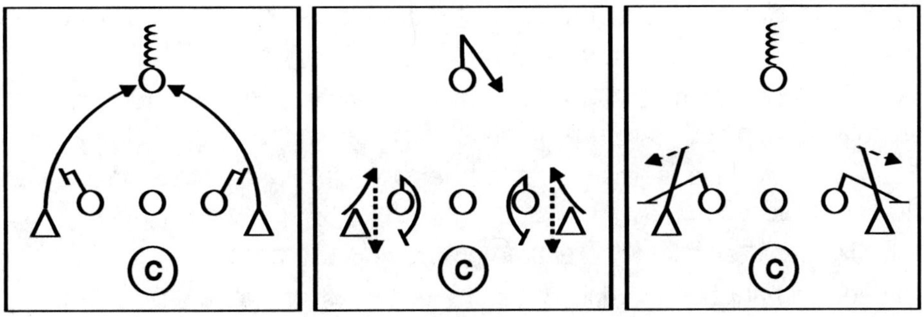

PASS DRAW SCREEN

Pass Rush Versus Pop-Up Dummies Drill

Greg Robinson
Head Coach, Syracuse University

Objective: To develop agility and speed. Incorporated are skills related to rushing, and stripping the footballs from and tackling the quarterback.

Equipment Needed: Six pop-up bags and footballs

Description:

- Align four pop-up bags five yards apart and in a vertical plane to a selected yard line. Place two additional pop-up bags one yard beyond and one yard to the right and to the left of the last bag (see the diagram).
- Align a row of defensive linemen one yard outside and two yards from the first bag.
- The coach stands one yard in front of the row of bags.
- On the coach's command, the first lineman drives from his three-point stance, executes a chop-and-rip technique on the first bag, and then sprints to the next bag.
- Again, the defensive lineman executes the chop-and-rip technique on the alternate side of the second bag.
- The previous description is executed on the next two bags.
- The lineman finishes the drill by turning either left or right after the last bag and executing a tackle and ball-strip technique on the bag on that side.
- The drill continues until all linemen have had a sufficient number of repetitions from both a left and a right alignment.

Coaching Points:

- Always check to see that the defensive linemen are in their proper stances before starting the drill.
- Insist that the drill be conducted at full speed.
- Instruct the defensive linemen as to the proper execution of the chop-and-rip technique.
- Emphasize the importance of staying low while moving through the bags.

Safety Considerations:

- Proper warm-up should precede the drill.
- Full equipment should be worn.
- The drill area should be clear of all foreign articles.
- Instruct the linemen in the proper fundamentals and techniques of safe tackling.

Variations:

- The drill can be used as an agility and speed drill for all pass-rush positions.
- Vary the distance between the bags.
- Use a club-and-rip, bob-and-squat, or a spin technique at the different bags.

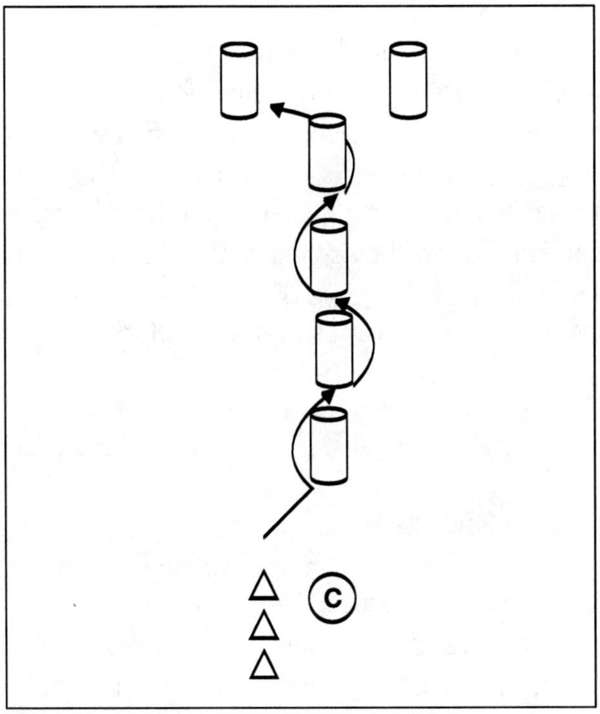

Hoop Drill

Tim Stowers
Head Coach, University of Rhode Island

Objective: To develop agility and speed. Incorporated are skills related to rushing the passer.

Equipment Needed: Two hoops (10 feet in diameter), two cones, and a football

Description:

- Place two hoops side-by-side on a selected yard line. Seven yards separate the two hoops. Place a cone one-and-a-half yards outside and just below the bottom of each hoop (see the diagram).
- Align a defensive lineman just inside each cone.
- Other linemen stand adjacent to the drill area.
- The coach, holding a football, is positioned between the two hoops (see the diagram).
- On the coach's cadence and simulated ball snap, the first two defensive linemen drive from their stance and run completely around the hoop.
- The two linemen finish the drill by sprinting past the cone.
- The drill continues until all defensive linemen have had a sufficient number of repetitions, running around the cones from each of the hoop stations.

Coaching Points:

- Always check to see that the defensive linemen are in their proper stances before starting the drill.
- Insist that the drill be conducted at full speed.
- Instruct the linemen to maintain a tight lean to the inside as they circle the hoops with their heads up and eyes focused straight ahead.
- Emphasize the importance of always keeping the arms pumping.
- Insist that the defensive linemen finish the drill by sprinting past the cone.

Safety Considerations:

- Proper warm-up should precede the drill.
- The drill area should be clear of all foreign articles.
- Alert defensive linemen who are waiting to perform the drill to stay clear of the drill-finish area.

Variations:

- Place two hoops in a figure-eight alignment with a two-yard separation, and have defensive linemen run a figure-eight pattern around the hoops.
- In ending the drill, the coach can set up a quarterback sack (pop-up bag) and a fumble-recovery situation.

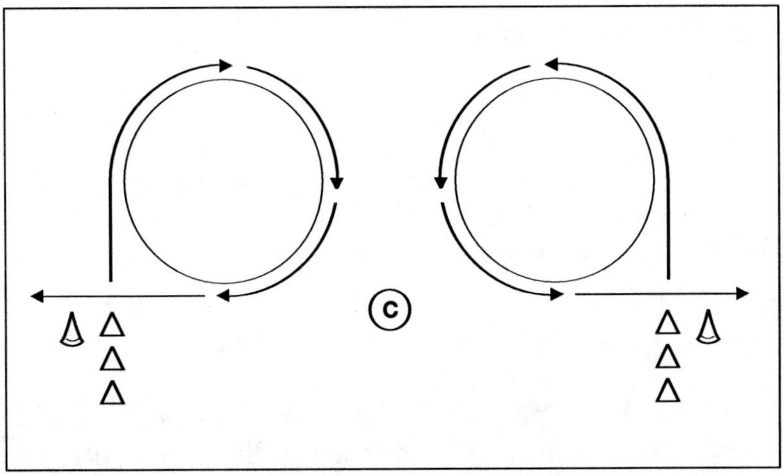

Wall Sprints Drill

Jerry Palmieri
Assistant Coach, New York Giants

Objective: To develop proper leg drive.

Equipment Needed: A sturdy vertical structure (such as a wall) with a line painted on the ground four feet from the wall.

Description:

- Align a row of defensive linemen five yards apart and on the painted line. Shorter linemen may need to position their feet closer to the wall, while taller linemen may need to position their feet farther behind the line.
- The coach stands adjacent to the row of linemen.
- On the coach's command, each lineman places his feet on the line and his hands on the wall (this placement should align the body at a 45-degree angle to the ground).
- On the coach's command, ("Step 1"), each lineman raises the right knee, forward and up, until a maximum height is reached so that the thigh is parallel to the ground and the heel is at the height of the left knee. The right ankle should be dorsiflexed (toe up) and the right heel under the hamstring, creating a positive shin angle with the ground.
- On the coach's second command ("Step 2"), each lineman drives the right leg down and back to the line, while simultaneously punching the left knee up, making sure the knees and feet point straight ahead and the ankles maintain dorsiflexion (toe up). Each lineman should execute four repetitions of these movements.
- On the coach's command ("Step 3"), each lineman drives his right leg forward immediately followed by driving his left leg forward. Each lineman should execute four repetitions of these movements.
- On the coach's command ("Step 4"), each lineman drives the right leg forward, then the left leg forward, and then right leg forward again. Each lineman should execute four repetitions of these movements.
- To finish the drill, each lineman punches and drives his legs continuously through the full range of motions of the wall sprints for five seconds, followed by a 10-second rest period. The rest period is followed by another five seconds of continuous wall sprints.

Coaching Points:

- Always check to see that the defensive linemen are in their correct body alignment on the wall.
- Instruct the linemen to create a straight line from the shoulders to the ankle in maintaining the 45-degree angle to the ground. Do not allow bending at the waist or the butt to stick up.
- Insist that all wall sprints be done first, with the linemen punching the knee forward and driving the legs back powerfully through the full range of motion.
- When executing the continuous sprints on the wall, make sure that the feet do not creep up but always hit the line.

Safety Considerations:

- Proper warm-up should precede the drill.
- The wall should be checked periodically for sturdiness.
- Make sure the line area is level.

Variations:

- The drill can be used for all positions.
- The drill can be executed with only one hand on the wall. When placing one on the wall, make sure that the drill participants pump the opposite arm in sequence with the right- and left-leg drives.

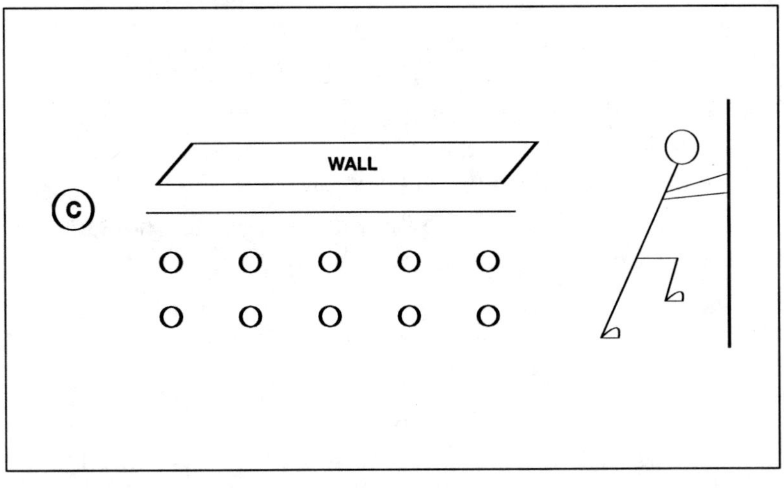

Eye and Reaction Drill

Bob Stoops
Head Coach, University of Oklahoma

Objective: To develop agility and speed. Incorporated are skills related to reading various offensive plays.

Equipment Needed: A fire hose and two hand shields

Description:

- Place a fire hose on a selected yard line.
- Position two defensive linemen in a three-point stance, with their upfoot against the fire hose. Two yards separate the two defensive linemen.
- Other defensive linemen stand adjacent to the drill area.
- The coach, with hand shields, is positioned at the midpoint and three yards in front of the two defensive linemen.
- On the coach's cadence and snap count, the two defensive linemen read and react to one of four hand-shield movements given by the coach: run straight ahead (see Diagram A), run away-redirect (see Diagram B), straight dropback pass (see Diagram C), and the draw-redirect (see Diagram D).
- The drill continues until all defensive linemen have had a sufficient number of repetitions of reading and reacting to the four plays presented in the previous description.

Coaching Points:

- Always check to see that the defensive linemen are aligned correctly and are in their proper stances.
- Insist that the drill be conducted at full speed.
- Instruct the defensive linemen as to the proper execution of reading and reacting to the four hand-shield movements given by the coach.

Safety Considerations:

- Proper warm-up should precede the drill.
- The drill area should be clear of all foreign articles.
- Maintain the designated distance between the pair of defensive linemen.

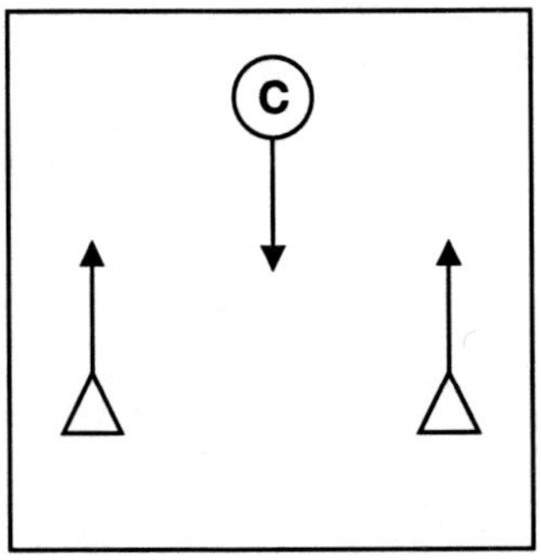

Diagram A

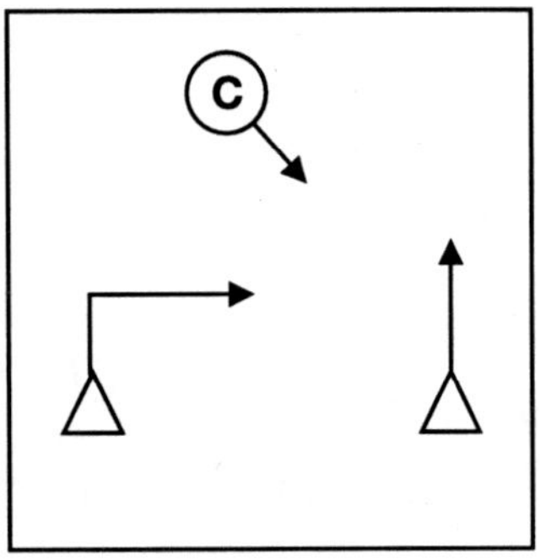

Diagram B

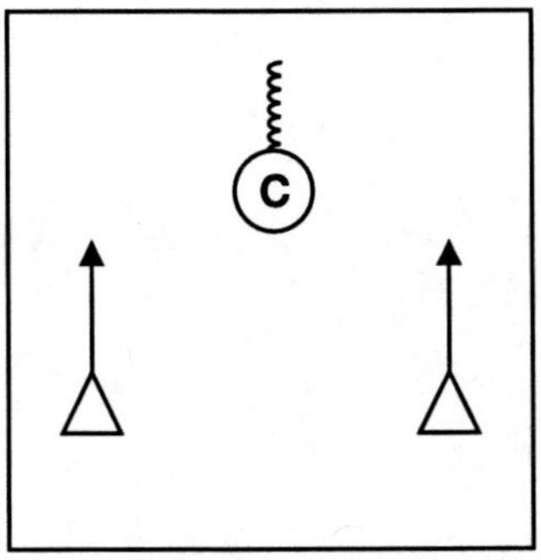

Diagram C

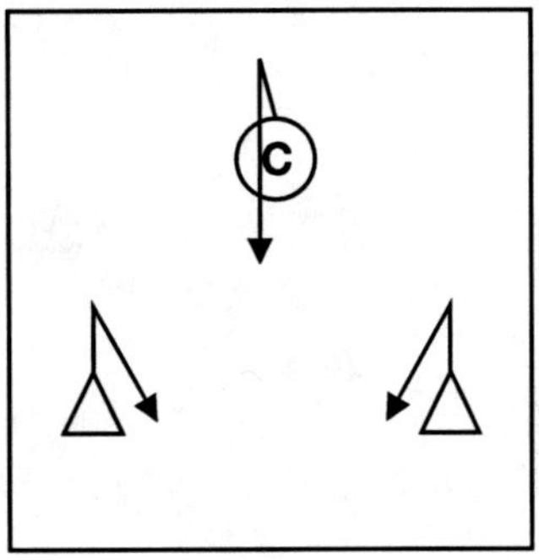

Diagram D

8

Linebacker Drills

Eye Opener Drill

Phillip Fulmer
Head Coach, University of Tennessee

Objective: To develop agility and speed. Incorporated are skills related to tackling a ballcarrier.

Equipment Needed: Five agility bags, two cones, and footballs

Description:

- Lay five agility bags two yards apart and perpendicular to a selected yard line.
- Align a row of linebackers three yards to the right of and three yards behind and facing the bags (see the diagram).
- Align a row of ballcarriers two yards to the left of and three yards behind and facing the bags.
- The coach stands adjacent to the drill area.
- On the coach's command, the first ballcarrier assumes the football ready position, and then runs laterally behind the bags. At the ballcarrier's discretion, the ballcarrier cuts up through any two of the bags.
- The first linebacker mirrors the run of the ballcarrier and executes a form tackle on the ballcarrier.
- The drill continues until all linebackers have had a sufficient number of repetitions from both a left and a right alignment.

Coaching Points:

- Always check to see that linebackers are in the football ready position before starting the drill.
- Insist that the drill be conducted at full speed.
- Instruct the linebackers to start the drill from a position one yard behind that of the ballcarrier.
- Instruct the linebackers to maintain a good football ready position throughout the drill.
- Make sure the linebackers maintain a good body position on the backside hip of the ballcarrier, and that they always approach the ballcarrier from an inside-out position, thus taking away the cutback angle.
- Insist that the linebackers practice the proper fundamentals and techniques of safe tackling.

Safety Considerations:

- It is imperative that proper warm-up precede the drill.
- The drill area should be clear of all foreign articles.
- Instruct all linebackers about the proper fundamentals and techniques of safe tackling.
- The coach should closely monitor the intensity of the drill.
- The coach should watch for and eliminate all unacceptable match-ups as to size and athletic ability.

Variations:

- Have the linebackers and ballcarriers thud up and back off and thud up and back off again through the different paired bags.
- Have the ballcarriers run back and forth behind the bags before cutting up through a pair of bags.
- The drill can be used for all tackling positions.

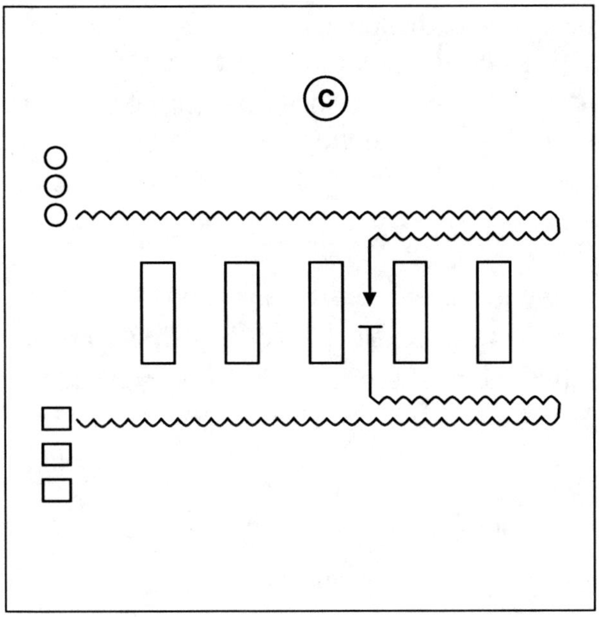

Star Drill

Tim Brewster
Head Coach, University of Minnesota

Objective: To develop agility and speed. Incorporated are skills related to changing directions.

Equipment Needed: Five cones

Description:

- Place four cones five yards apart to form a square. Place a fifth cone in the middle of the square to form a star (see the diagram).
- Align a row of linebackers five yards behind and at the midpoint of the bottom of the star.
- The coach stands on the opposite side of the star and faces the row of linebackers.
- On the coach's command, the first linebacker sprints to the middle cone and fires his feet.
- The coach points to one of the four corner cones and the linebacker sprints to that cone and then turns and sprints back to the center cone and again fires his feet.
- After the linebacker completes three directional signal movements, the coach gives one last command ("Burst"), and the linebacker sprints past the coach.
- The drill continues until all linebackers have had a sufficient number of repetitions.

Coaching Points:

- Always check to see that linebackers are firing their feet before starting the drill.
- Instruct the linebackers to maintain the proper body alignment throughout the drill.
- Emphasize the importance of executing short and quick bursts of speed.
- Insist that the linebackers finish the drill by sprinting past the coach.

Safety Considerations:

- Proper warm-up should precede the drill.
- The drill area should be clear of all foreign articles.

Variations:

- The drill can be used as a general agility and speed drill for all positions.
- Vary the distances between the cones.

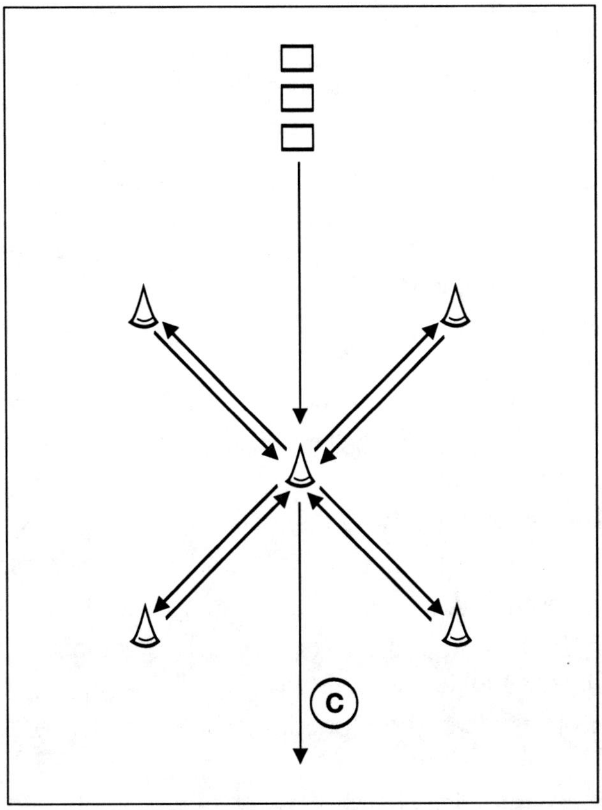
C

Bulldog Shuffle Drill

Steve Patton
Head Coach, Gardner-Webb University

Objective: To develop agility and speed. Incorporated are skills related to changing directions.

Equipment Needed: Five agility bags

Description:

- Lay five agility bags one yard apart and perpendicular to a selected yard line.
- Position a linebacker, in a football ready position, one yard from and facing sideways to the row of bags.
- Other linebackers stand adjacent to the drill area.
- The coach stands at the midpoint of and faces the row of bags.
- On the coach's command, the first linebacker shuffles laterally over the bags.
- When reaching the far end of the bags, the linebacker plants his outside foot and transitions his lateral shuffle back over the bags to the starting point.
- The linebacker plants his outside foot, turns, and sprints over and five yards past the bags.
- The drill continues until all linebackers have had a sufficient number of repetitions, starting from both the left and the right sides of the drill area.

Coaching Points:

- Always check to see that the linebackers are in the football ready position before starting the drill.
- Insist that the drill be conducted at full speed.
- Emphasize the importance of making quick transitions with each change of direction.
- Make sure all linebackers maintain the proper body alignment as they shuffle over the bags.
- Insist that the linebackers keep their heads up and eyes focused straight ahead.
- Instruct the linebackers to always plant with the outside foot with each transition.
- Insist that the linebackers finish the drill by sprinting five yards past the last bag.

Safety Considerations:

- Proper warm-up should precede the drill.
- The drill area should be clear of all foreign articles.

Variations:

- The drill can be used as an agility and speed drill for all positions.
- Add a pass catch or a fumble recovery in finishing the drill.

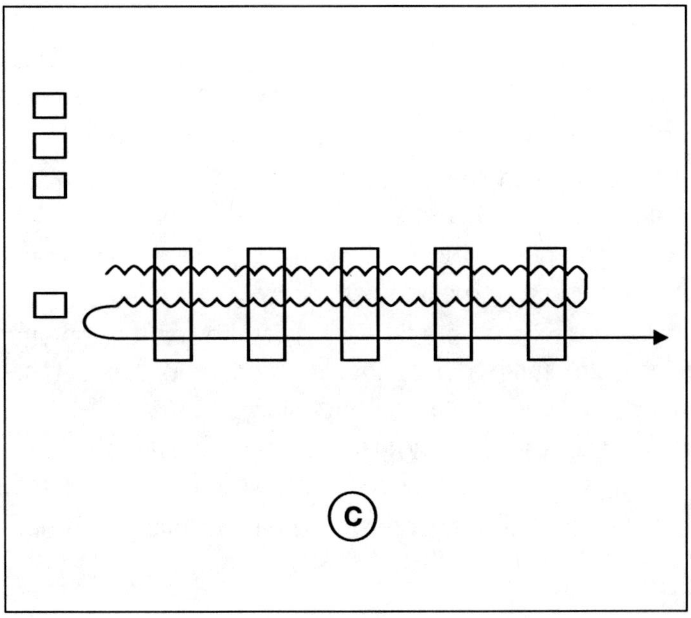

Inside/Outside Tackle Drill

Troy Calhoun
Head Coach, United States Air Force Academy

Objective: To develop agility and speed. Incorporated are skill related to tackling a ballcarrier.

Equipment Needed: Footballs

Description:

- Align two rows of linebackers three yards apart on a sideline. Designate one row as ballcarriers and the other as linebackers (tacklers) (see the diagram).
- The coach stands at various points adjacent to the drill area.
- On the coach's command, the first ballcarrier runs and jogs in a straight line across the football field, changing his speed at different intervals.
- The first linebacker mirrors the path of the first ballcarriers, maintaining a good inside-out relationship to the ballcarrier.
- When the ballcarrier reaches the far hash mark, he can turn up and try to beat the linebacker by outrunning him to the corner, or he can cut back behind the linebacker as the linebacker makes the tackle.
- The linebacker and ballcarrier jog to the far sideline and change rows. The linebacker becomes the ballcarrier and the ballcarrier becomes the linebacker.
- The drill continues until all linebackers have had a sufficient number of repetitions.

Coaching Points:

- Instruct the linebackers to always maintain an inside-out relationship with ballcarrier. The linebacker should never be in front of or even with the ballcarrier, and never more than two yards behind the ballcarrier.
- Make sure all linebackers maintain good body alignment throughout the drill.
- Instruct the linebackers about the proper fundamentals and techniques of safe tackling.

Safety Considerations:

- Proper warm-up should precede the drill.
- The drill area (especially the sideline areas) should be clear of all foreign articles.
- Full equipment should be worn.

Variations:

- Vary the distance between the two rows of drill participants.
- The drill can be used for all tackling positions.

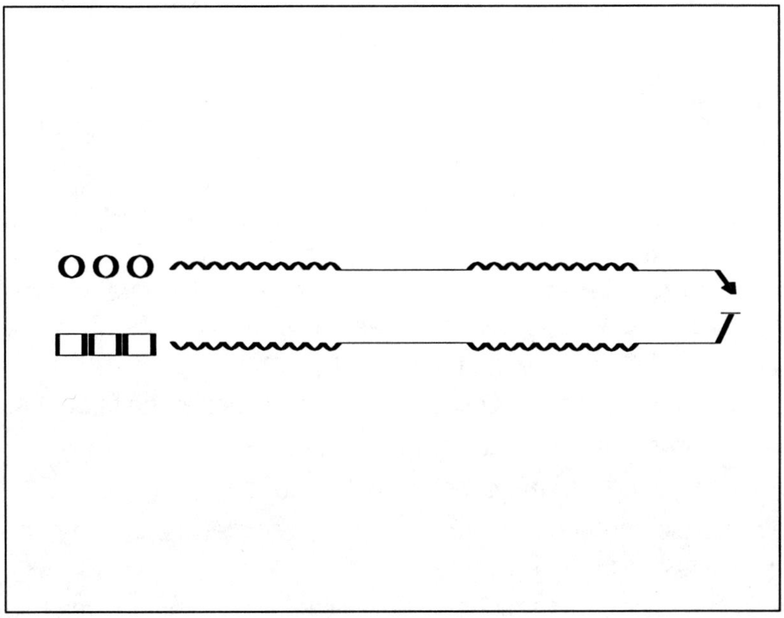

Three-Cone Wave Drill

Shane Burnham
Assistant Coach, Elon University

Objective: To develop agility and speed. Incorporated are skills related to changing directions.

Equipment Needed: Ten cones

Description:

- Align two rows of cones five yards apart. Three yards should separate the cones in each row. Place three additional cones in a row behind and just to the left of the midpoint between the two rows of cones. Theses cones are also separated by three yards. A final cone is placed three yards in front of and at the midpoint between the two rows of cones (see the diagram).
- Position three linebackers adjacent to each of the cones at the back of the drill area.
- Other linebackers stand adjacent to the drill area.
- The coach stands behind the cone at the front of the drill area.
- On the coach's command ("Feet"), the three linebackers assume the football ready position and fast fire their feet.
- On the coach's command ("Go"), the three linebackers sprint to the corresponding cones that form the two rows of cones (see the diagram).
- The coach points to the cones on either the left or right side of the drill area, and the three linebackers shuffle to that cone and then shuffle back to the center. This pointing and shuffling is repeated several times.
- On the coach's command ("Feet"), the three linebackers again fast fire their feet.
- On the coach's command, ("Finish"), the three linebackers finish the drill by sprinting past the coach.
- The drill continues until all linebackers have had a sufficient number of repetitions.

Coaching Points:

- Always check to see that linebackers are in the football ready position before starting the drill.
- Insist that the drill be conducted at full speed.
- Emphasize the importance of maintaining the proper football ready position throughout the drill.
- Insist that all linebackers finish the drill by sprinting past the coach.

Safety Considerations:

- Proper warm-up should precede the drill.
- The drill area should be clear of all foreign articles.

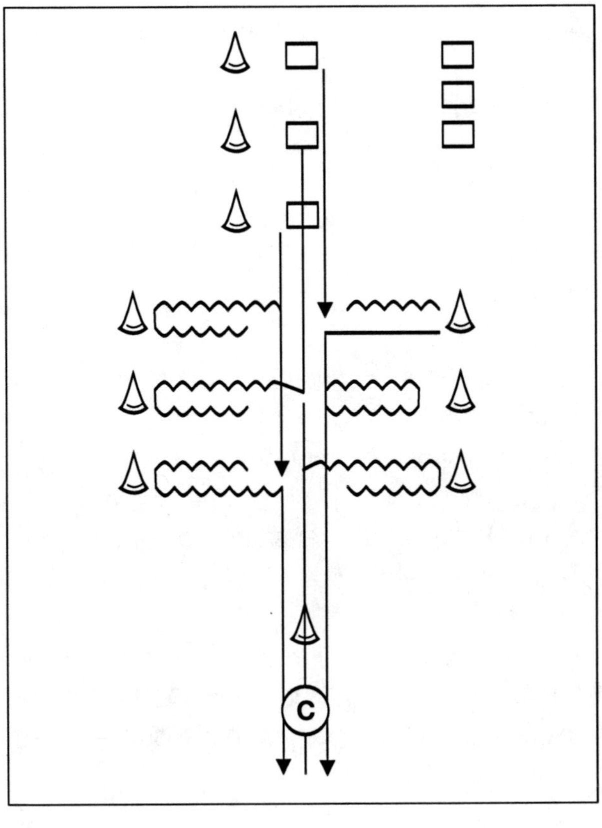

Four-Cone X Drill

Bob Sanders
Assistant Coach, Green Bay Packers

Objective: To develop agility and speed. Incorporated are many of the movement patterns a linebacker need to perfect, as well as skills related to intercepting a pass.

Equipment Needed: Four cones and a football

Description:

- Align four cones (A, B, C, and D) 10 yards apart to form a square (see the diagram).
- Position a row of linebackers adjacent to cone A.
- The coach, holding a football, is positioned five yards in front of and outside of cone D.
- On the coach's command, the first linebacker backpedals past cone B, turns, faces the inside, and shuffles past cone C.
- The linebacker turns and sprints to cone D.
- From cone D, the linebacker opens (as in a zone pass drop) and moves diagonally to cone B. From cone B, the linebacker sprints to cone A.
- From cone A, the linebacker again opens (as in a zone pass drop) and moves to cone C.
- The linebacker sprints toward cone D, catches the pass thrown by the coach, and finishes the drill by sprinting five yards past the coach.
- The drill continues until all linebackers have had a sufficient number of repetitions.

Coaching Points:

- Always check to see that the linebackers are in the football ready position before starting the drill.
- Insist that the drill be conducted at full speed.
- Instruct the linebackers to execute all movements through the drill (backpedal, shuffle, sprint, and zone pass drop) in the proper manner.
- Insist that the linebackers finish the drill by catching the thrown pass and sprinting five yards past the coach.

Safety Considerations:

- Proper warm-up should precede the drill.
- The drill area should be clear of all foreign articles.
- Alert the linebackers who are waiting to perform the drill to stay clear of the cone-A area when linebackers are moving around that cone.

Variations:

- The drill can be used as a defensive back drill.
- Vary the distances between the cones.
- Vary the sequence of some of the movements.

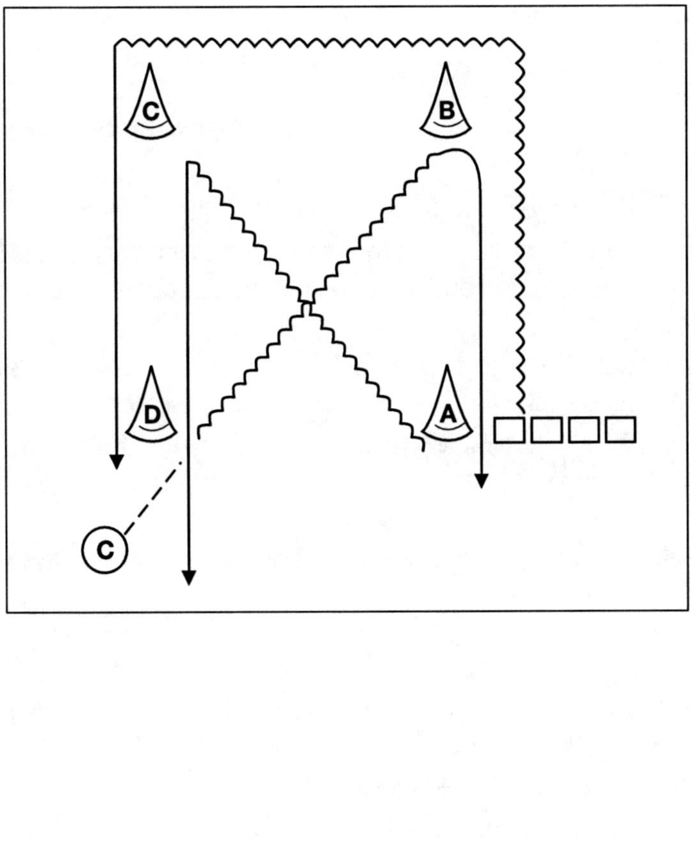

Lateral Tire Shuffle/Pro-Agility Tire Relay

Al Golden
Head Coach, Temple University

Objective: To develop agility and speed. Incorporated skills related to maintaining a great football position.

Equipment Needed: Two tires and three cones

Description:

- Place three cones in a straight line five yards apart and on three separate yard lines (see the diagram).
- Position two linebackers facing one another three yards apart on the yard line adjacent to the middle cone. Other linebackers from equal rows (teams) behind the first two linebackers.
- Position a tire in a lateral alignment in front of each of the first two performing linebackers.
- Align a coach at each yard line at the two end cones.
- On the coach's command, blowing the whistle, each linebacker rolls his tire to each of the outside yard lines (end cones) and then back to the middle yard line (middle cone).
- The first two linebackers go to the back of their team's row and sit down as the next two linebackers take their position adjacent to the two tires.
- The drill continues until all linebackers have taken their turn in rolling the tire to each of the outside yard lines (end cones) and then back to the middle yard line (middle cone).
- The linebackers' relay team that wins the best out of three relays is declared the winner.

Coaching Points:

- Always check to see that the linebackers are in the football ready position before starting the drill.
- Insist that the drill be conducted at full speed.
- Instruct all linebackers to maintain the proper football position throughout the drill.
- Make sure all linebackers touch each outside yard line (cone) with the tire before moving back to the middle yard line (cone).

Safety Considerations:

- Proper warm-up should precede the drill.
- Make sure all linebackers start the drill by rolling the tires in the same direction.

Variations:

- Vary the distances between the cones.
- The drill can be used as a general agility and speed drill for all positions.

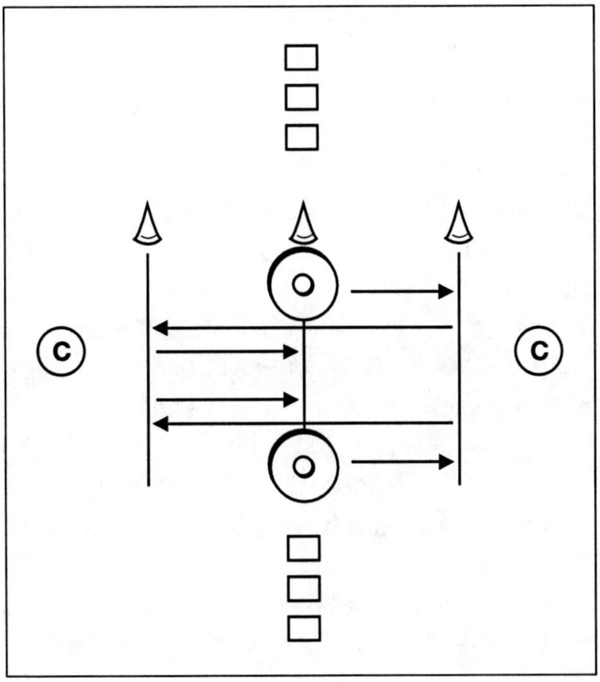

Hoops Dips Drill

Jud Keim
Assistant Coach, Pacific Lutheran University

Objective: To develop agility and speed. Incorporated are skills related to rushing the passer from the outside linebacker positions with special emphasis on the dipping of the inside shoulder.

Equipment Needed: Two hoops (10 feet in diameter), four rags, and a football

Description:

- Place two hoops, one on top of the other, adjacent to a selected yard line. One yard separates the two hoops. Place four rags, one each, just inside of the edges and at the midpoint of each of the hoops (see the diagram).
- Align a row of outside linebackers at the midpoint of the lower hoop.
- The coach, holding a football, is positioned just inside of the lower hoop and facing the row of outside linebackers.
- On the coach's cadence and simulated ball snap, the first linebacker drives from his stance and runs the hoops in a figure-eight pattern.
- As the first linebacker approaches each rag, he bends down and scoops up the rags with the inside hand to simulate lowering his pads as if to dip and rip a blocker.
- After scooping up each rag, the linebacker tosses the rag to the sky.
- The first linebacker finishes the drill by sprinting five yards past the midpoint of the lower hoop.
- The drill continues until all outside linebackers have had a sufficient number of repetitions, running the hoops from both a clockwise and counter-clockwise direction.

Coaching Points:

- Always check to see that outside linebackers are in their proper stances before starting the drill.
- Insist that the drill be conducted at full speed.
- Emphasize the importance of maintaining an inside body lean and running tight to the circle in moving around the hoops.
- In picking up the rags, instruct the outside linebacker to bend at the knees and exaggerate the full reach as they scoop up the rags (they should scrape their knuckles on the grass).
- Insist that the linebackers finish the drill by sprinting five yards past the finish line.

Safety Considerations:

- Proper warm-up should precede the drill.
- The drill area should be clear of all foreign articles.
- Alert the drill participants who are waiting to perform the drill to stay clear of the drill-finish area.
- In introducing the drill for the first time, the drill should be conducted at half speed.

Variations:

- Start a second outside linebacker at a designated distance behind the first linebacker to create a chase situation.
- The drill can be used by all pass-rush positions.

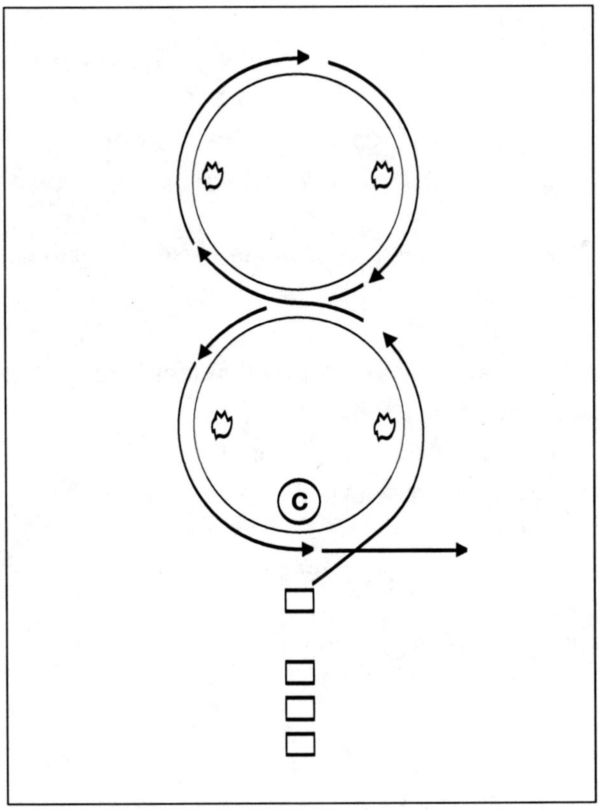

Cone Drill

Sylvester Croon
Head Coach, Mississippi State University

Objective: To develop agility and speed. Incorporated are skills related to the execution of the backpedal and intercepting a pass.

Equipment Needed: Four cones and a football

Description:

- Place four cones (A, B, C, and D) 10 yards apart to form a square (see the diagram).
- Align a row of linebackers 10 yards below cone A at the base of the square.
- The coach, holding a football, is positioned at the midpoint and five yards behind the base of the square.
- On the coach's command, the first linebacker backpedals from his usual stance past cone A. At cone A, the linebacker turns and sprints past the front of cone B.
- The linebacker backpedals past cone C and then sprints past the back of cone D.
- The linebacker backpedals 10 yards downfield and intercepts the pass thrown by the coach.
- The linebacker finishes the drill by sprinting past the outside area of the square.

Coaching Points:

- Always check to see that the linebackers are in their proper stances before starting the drill.
- Insist that the drill be conducted at full speed.
- Instruct the linebackers to maintain the proper body alignment as they move through the cone area.
- Emphasize the importance of always keeping the head up with eyes focused straight ahead at all times.
- Insist that the linebackers secure the football and sprint past the square after intercepting the pass.

Safety Considerations:

- Proper warm-up should precede the drill.
- The drill area should be clear of all foreign articles.
- Alert the linebackers as they sprint to finish the drill to stay outside the drill area.

Variations:

- The drill can be used as defensive back drill.
- Vary the distance between the cones.

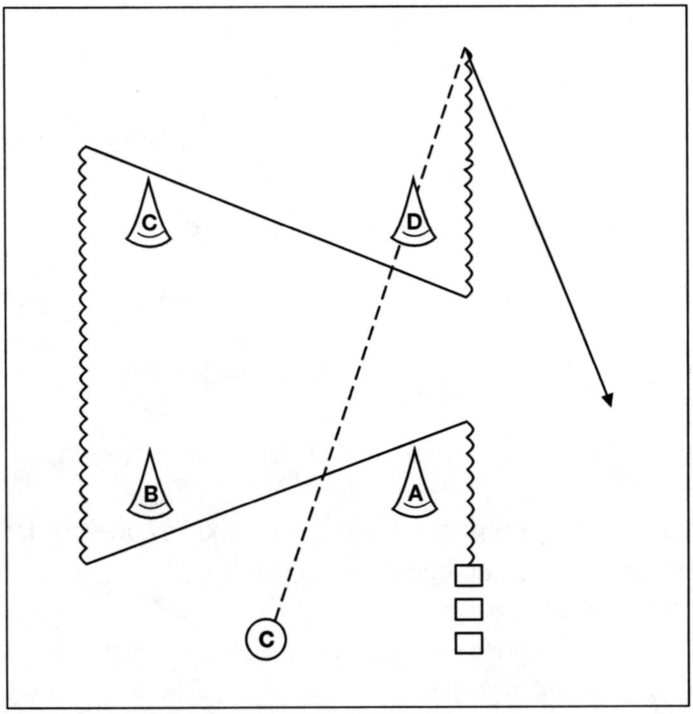

Agility Bag Drill

Vic Shealy
Assistant Coach, University of Nevada, Las Vegas

Objective: To develop agility and speed. Incorporated are skills related to intercepting a pass.

Equipment Needed: Five agility bags and footballs

Description:

- Lay five agility bags one yard apart and perpendicular to a selected yard line (see the diagram).
- Align a row of linebackers one yard in front and in a sideways alignment to the row of bags.
- The coach, holding a football, is positioned five yards in front of and at the midpoint of the bag area.
- On the coach's command, the first linebacker assumes the football ready position beside the first bag.
- On the coach's second command, the linebacker shuffles over and through the bags.
- The linebacker plants his outside foot, backpedals for five yards, and intercepts the pass thrown by the coach.
- In finishing the drill, the linebacker tucks the intercepted pass away and sprints five yards back past the bag area.
- The drill continues until all linebackers have had a sufficient number of repetitions shuffling both left and right over and through the bags.

Coaching Points:

- Always check to see that the linebackers are in the football ready position before starting the drill.
- Insist that the drill be conducted at full speed.
- Make sure the linebackers maintain the proper body alignment as they shuffle over and through the bags.
- Insist that the linebackers keep their heads up and eyes focused straight ahead throughout the drill.
- In finishing the drill, insist that the linebackers sprint five yards past the bag area.

Safety Considerations:

- Proper warm-up should precede the drill.
- The drill area should be clear of all foreign articles.

Variation:

- The drill can be used as defensive back drill.

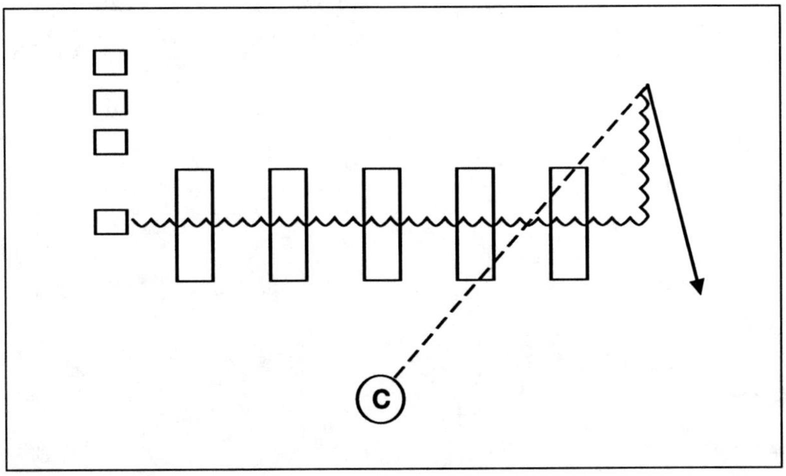

9

Defensive End Drills

Speed Rush Drill

Greg Schiano
Head Coach, Rutgers University

Objective: To develop agility and speed. Incorporated are skills related to rushing the passer.

Equipment Needed: A hoop (10 feet in diameter), four cones, and a football

Description:

- Place a hoop on a selected yard line.
- Place four cones (A, B, C, and D) at various relationships to the hoop. Cone A is placed four yards below and to the left of the hoop. Cone B is placed just inside the hoop and at the midpoint on the left side of the hoop. Cone C is placed just past the right bend at the top of the hoop, and cone D is placed in the same vertical plane as cone C and beside cone A.
- Position a row of defensive ends behind cone A.
- The coach, holding a football, is positioned adjacent to the row of defensive ends.
- On the coach's cadence and ball snap, the first defensive end explodes from his stance and drives to cone B, executing a rip technique with the inside arm.
- The defensive end runs to cone C, plants the outside foot, and sprints past cone D.
- The drill continues until all defensive ends have had a sufficient number of repetitions, moving in both directions around the hoop.

Coaching Points:

- Always check to see that the defensive ends are in their proper stances before starting the drill.
- Insist that the drill be conducted at full speed.
- Instruct the defensive ends, at cone B, to make sure that they rip on air and run tight to the hoop with the proper inside body lean.
- Instruct the defensive ends to plant the outside foot at cone C and sprint at a 90-degree angle past cone D.

Safety Considerations:

- Proper warm-up should precede the drill.
- The drill area should be clear of all foreign articles.
- Instruct the defensive ends as to the proper techniques of executing all phases of the drill.

Variations:

- The drill can be used by all pass-rush positions.
- Position a coach with an arm pad at cone B.
- Have the defensive ends execute a 360-degree turn at cone C and circle the hoop back to cone A.

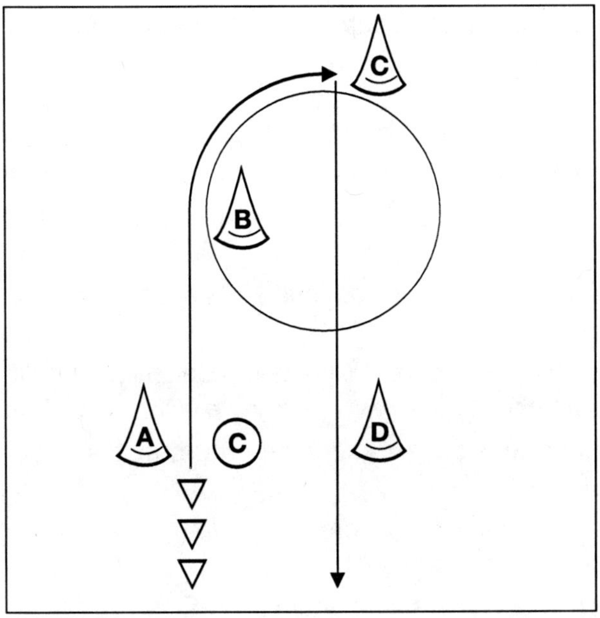

Diamond Drill

Joe Tiller
Head Coach, Purdue University

Objective: To develop agility and speed. Incorporated are skills related to the execution of the rip-and-club technique and changing directions.

Equipment Needed: Four cones, a pop-up dummy and a football

Description:

- Place four cones (A, B, C, and D) 10 yards apart to form a diamond. Place a pop-up dummy, with a holder, in the middle of the diamond (see the diagram).
- Align a row of defensive ends behind cone A, which forms the lower point of the diamond.
- The coach, holding a football, is positioned in a quarterback relationship to the row of defensive ends.
- On the coach's cadence and ball snap, the first defensive end drives from his stance and sprints to the pop-up dummy, where he executes a club and rip technique.
- The defensive end runs around the pop-up dummy and proceeds to and circles cone B.
- After the defensive end circles cone B, he returns to the pop-up dummy and repeats the rip-and-club technique.
- The previous description is repeated for cones C and D.
- The defensive end finishes the drill by sprinting past cone A.
- The drill continues until all defensive ends have a sufficient number of repetitions.

Coaching Points:

- Always check to see that the defensive ends are in their proper stance before starting the drill.
- Insist that the drill be conducted at full speed.
- Instruct the defensive ends that after circling each cone and the pop-up dummy, they should work for a 90-degree angle by planting and cutting off the outside foot and pointing the inside foot in the direction of the next cone.
- Emphasize the importance of taking long steps in running to the pop-up dummy and accelerating when driving to the cones.
- Insist that the defensive end finish the drill by sprinting past cone A.

Safety Considerations:

- Proper warm-up should precede the drill.
- The drill area should be clear of all foreign articles.
- Alert defensive ends who are waiting to perform the drill to stay well clear of the drill-finish area. (This directive also includes the coach.)

Variations:

- Eliminate the rip-and-club technique, and use as a general speed and agility drill for all positions.
- Vary the distances between the cones.
- Position a coach, holding an arm shield, in the middle of the diamond, and have the defensive ends knock his hands down.

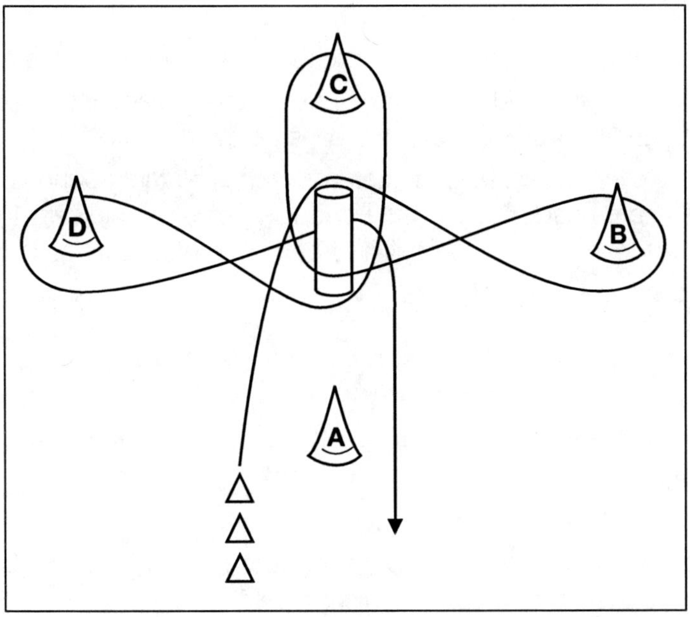

Bag Competition Drill

Jerry Kill
Head Coach, Southern Illinois University

Objective: To develop agility and speed. Incorporated are factors related to competitiveness.

Equipment Needed: Eight agility bags and one cone

Description:

- Align two parallel rows of agility bags separated by five yards. The agility bags in each row are placed one yard apart. A cone is placed between the two rows at the start/finish position of the drill (see the diagram).
- Position equally divided rows of defensive ends in a front-facing alignment to each row of bags.
- The coach stands at the far end of the drill area between the two rows of bags.
- On the coach's command, the first defensive end in each row explodes from his stance and runs over and through the bags on their side.
- After moving over the last bag, the defensive ends hit the ground with their chests, get up, and sprint back between the two rows of bags and past the cone at the finish line. After completing the drill, the defensive ends change lines.
- The drill continues until all defensive ends have had a sufficient number of repetitions.

Coaching Points:

- Always check to see that the defensive ends are in their proper stances before starting the drill.
- Insist that the drill be conducted at full speed.
- In running over and through the bags, instruct the defensive ends to keep their heads up and their eyes focused straight ahead.
- Emphasize the importance of getting off the ground quickly after hitting the ground with the chest.
- To increase competitiveness, the coach should pair defensive ends that are equal in speed and athletic ability.

Safety Considerations:

- Proper warm-up should precede the drill.
- The drill area should be clear of all foreign articles.
- Alert defensive ends who are waiting to perform the drill to stay well clear of the drill-finish area.

Variations:

- Vary the distance between the bags.
- Have the defensive end move over and through the bags in different ways (shuffle, carioca, etc.).
- The drill can be used as a speed and agility drill by all positions.

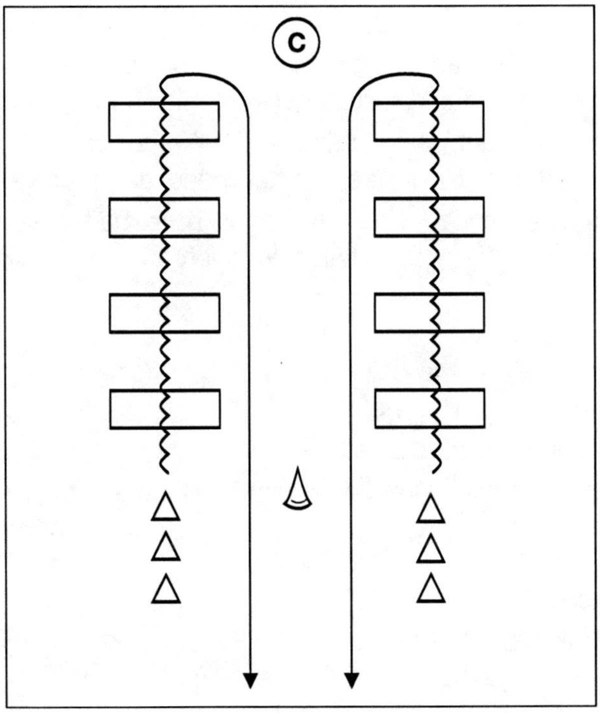

Speedy Pass-Rush Drill

Pat Sullivan
Head Coach, Samford University

Objective: To develop agility and speed. Incorporated are skills related to rushing the passer.

Equipment Needed: Four cones, a pop-up dummy, and a football

Description:

- Place four cones to form a rectangle. The width of the rectangle is seven yards, and the height of the rectangle is four yards (see the diagram).
- Align a row of defensive ends outside of each of the two cones that form the base of the rectangle.
- The coach, holding a football, is positioned at the midpoint of the base of the rectangle.
- On the coach's cadence and snap count, the first defensive lineman in each row explodes from his stance and rushes upfield to the front cone.
- At the front cone, the defensive ends execute the designated rush technique (rip, swim, club, etc.), turn to the inside, run full speed, and touch the pop-up dummy.
- The drill continues until all defensive ends have had a sufficient number of repetitions of rushing the passer both from a left and a right alignment.

Coaching Points:

- Always check to see that the defensive ends are aligned correctly and are in their proper stance before starting the drill.
- Insist that the drill be conducted at full speed.
- Instruct the defensive ends as to the proper mechanics in the execution of the (rip, swim, club) technique.

Safety Considerations:

- Proper warm-up should precede the drill.
- The drill area should be clear of all foreign articles.

Variations:

- Vary the width and height of the rectangle.
- The drill can be used by other pass-rushing positions.

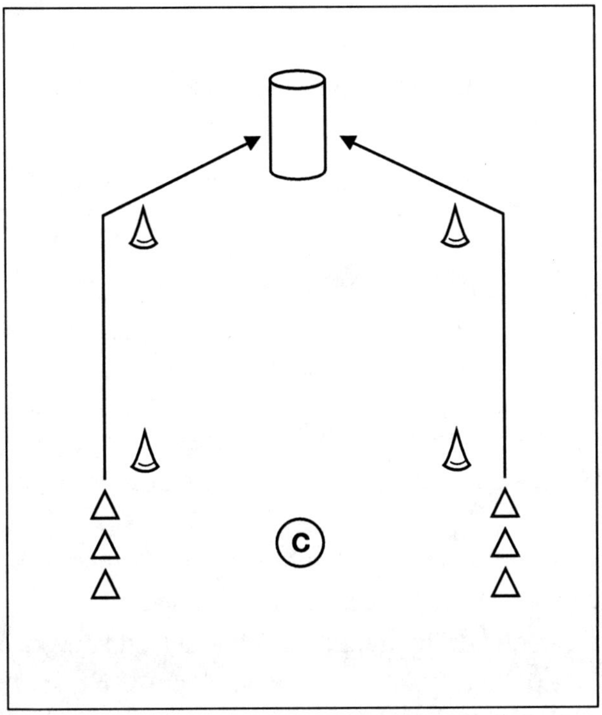
C

Three-Bag Agility Drill

David Elson
Head Coach, Western Kentucky University

Objective: To develop agility and speed. Incorporated are skills related to changing directions.

Equipment Needed: Six agility bags and two cones

Description:

- Place two sets of three agility bags five yards apart on a selected yard line. The agility bags in each set are placed two yards apart.
- Place a cone five yards in front of the bag on the outside of each set of bags (see the diagram).
- Position a defensive end beside the first bag of each set.
- Other defensive ends stand adjacent to the drill area.
- The coach is positioned at the midpoint of the drill and seven yards upfield.
- On the coach's command ("Set"), the first two defensive ends assume the football ready position, buzzing their feet.
- On the coach's second command ("Go"), the first two defensive ends shuffle over and through the three bags and then redirect and shuffle back over the bags.
- The defensive ends drive off their back foot and sprint past the cone on their side.
- The drill continues until all defensives ends have had a sufficient number of repetitions.

Coaching Points:

- Always check to see that the defensive ends are in the proper football ready position before starting the drill.
- Insist that the drill be conducted at full speed.
- In executing the shuffle, make sure that the defensive ends maintain the proper body alignment with their heads up and eyes focused straight ahead.
- Instruct the defensive ends to place two feet in each hole when executing the shuffle.
- Insist that the defensive ends finish the drill by sprinting past the cones.

Safety Considerations:

- Proper warm-up should precede the drill.
- The drill area should be clear of all foreign articles.

Variations:

- Add additional agility bags.
- Move the finish line cones straight ahead instead of at an angle.
- The drill can be used as a general agility and speed drill for all positions.

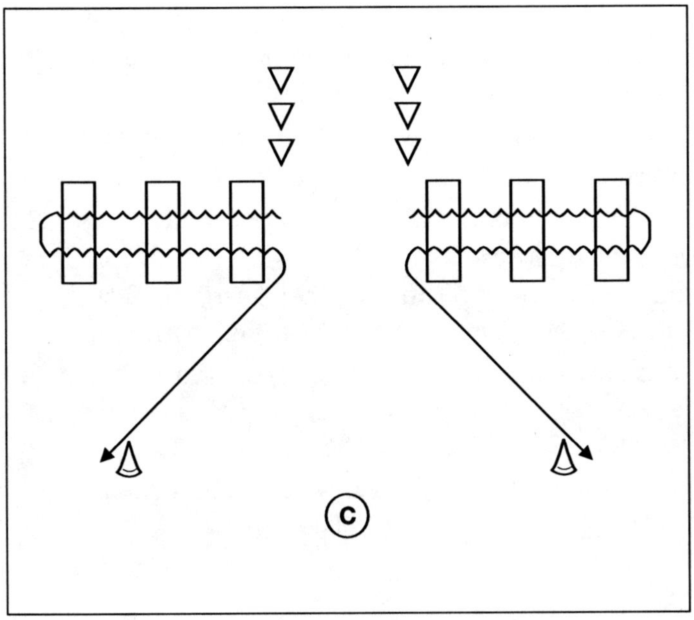

Change of Direction

Joe Tiller
Head Coach, Purdue University

Objective: To develop agility and speed. Incorporated are skills related to changing directions.

Equipment Needed: Four cones and a football

Description:

- Place two cones four feet apart on the five-yard line. Two additional cones are placed in front of these two cones on the one-yard line. A distance of 10 yards separates these two cones (see the diagram).
- Position a defensive end outside either of the cones on the five-yard line.
- Other defensive ends stand adjacent to the drill area.
- The coach, holding a football, stands on the one-yard line and at the midpoint of the two cones on the five-yard line.
- On the coach's cadence and simulated ball snap, the first defensive end drives from his sprinter's stance and runs straight at the coach.
- If the coach points his hand forward, the defensive end turns and sprints back through the two cones positioned on the five-yard line. If the coach points to the sideline, the defensive ends sprint past the cone on that side.
- The drill continues until all defensive ends have had a sufficient number of repetitions, starting from both five-yard-line cones.

Coaching Points:

- Always check to see that all defensive ends are in their sprinter's stance before starting the drill.
- Insist that the drill be conducted at full speed.
- Instruct defensive ends to focus on the football snap and to strive for a great get-off.
- Emphasize the importance of reacting to and changing directions quickly on the coach's signal.
- Insist that all defensive ends finish the drill by sprinting through the two cones on the five-yard line or past the designated cone on the one-yard line.

Safety Considerations:

- Proper warm-up should precede the drill.
- The drill area should be clear of all foreign articles.
- Defensive ends with knee and ankle problems should be exempt from this drill.
- When presenting this drill for the first time, the coach should caution the defensive ends not to run into the coach.

Variations:

- The drill can be used as a general agility and speed drill for all positions.
- Vary the distance between the five-yard line cones and coach.

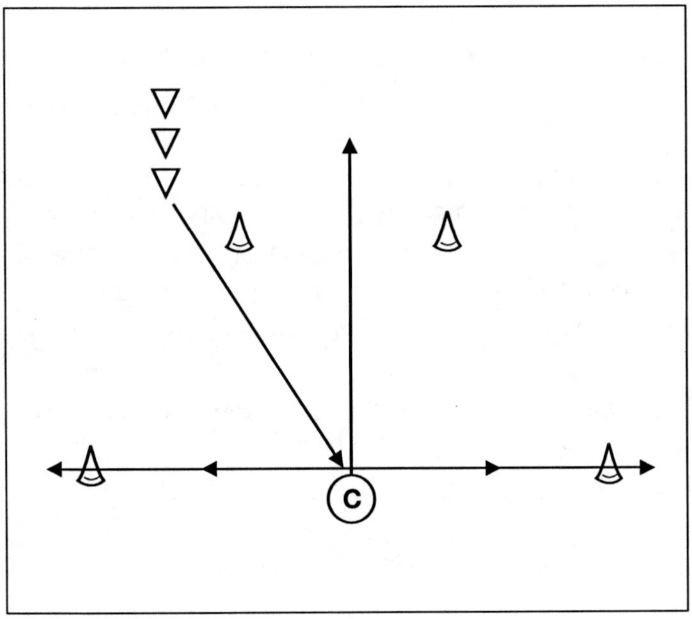

Shuffle Return Drill

Phil Bennett
Head Coach, Southern Methodist University

Objective: To develop agility and speed. Incorporated are skills related to assuming and maintaining the proper football ready position.

Equipment Needed: Four agility bags, two pop-up dummies, and a football

Description:

- Place four agility bags two yards apart on a selected yard line. Place a pop-up dummy five yards outside and at a 45-degree angle to the agility bag at each end of the bag area (see the diagram).
- Position a row of defensive ends behind the first agility bag.
- The coach, holding a football, stands at the midpoint of the bags and opposite the row of defensive lends.
- On the coach's command, the first defensive end drives from his three-point stance and assumes the football ready position, straddling the first bag.
- On the coach's cadence and simulated ball snap, the first defensive end shuffles over and through the bags (touching both feet in each hole).
- After shuffling over the last bag, the defensive end continues his shuffle back over the bags to the starting point.
- Upon finishing the return shuffle, the defensive end executes a rip technique through the pop-up dummy on that side.
- The defensive end finishes the drill by sprinting 10 yards upfield.
- The drill continues until all defensive ends have had a sufficient number of repetitions, starting from both a left and a right alignment.

Coaching Points:

- Always check to see that the defensive ends are in their three-point stances before starting the drill.
- Insist that the drill be conducted a full speed.
- Emphasize the importance of always maintaining the proper football position throughout the drill.
- Instruct the defensive ends to always keep their heads up and eyes focused straight ahead.
- Insist that all defensive ends finish the drill by executing the rip technique through the pop-up dummy and sprinting 10 yards upfield.

Safety Considerations:

- Proper warm-up should precede the drill.
- The drill area should be clear of all foreign articles.

Variations:

- The drill can be used for all defensive positions.
- Vary the number of bags.

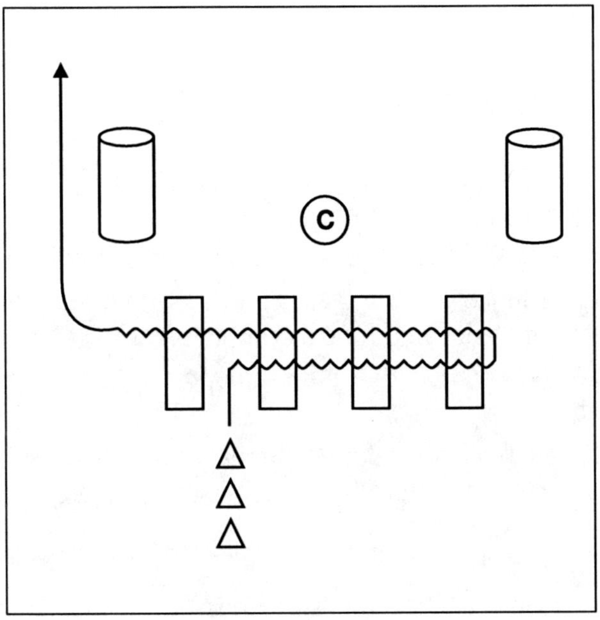

Red Raider Speed Loops

Rocky Rees
Head Coach, Shippensburg University

Objective: To develop agility and speed. Incorporated are skills related to rushing the passer.

Equipment Needed: A loop (12 feet in diameter), a cone and a football

Description:

- Place a loop adjacent to a selected yard line. Place a cone seven yards beyond and to the left of the top of the loop (see the diagram).
- Position a defensive end in a three-point stance at the midpoint of the left side of the loop.
- Other defensive ends stand adjacent to the drill area.
- A coach, holding a football, is positioned in a center relationship to the defensive end.
- On the coach's cadence and simulated ball snap, the first defensive end drives from his three-point stance and runs around the loop.
- As the defensive end completes his run around the loop, he finishes the drill by sprinting past the upfield cone.
- The drill continues until all defensive ends have had a sufficient number of repetitions, circling the loop from both a left and a right alignment.

Coaching Points:

- Always check to see that the defensive ends are in their proper stance before starting the drill.
- Insist that the drill be conducted at full speed.
- Instruct the defensive ends to lean close to the inside of the loop, dipping the inside shoulder as they circle the loop.
- Insist that the defensive ends finish the drill by sprinting past the upfield cone.

Safety Considerations:

- Proper warm-up should precede the drill.
- The drill area should be clear of all foreign articles.
- This drill should not be used when the ground is slippery.

Variations:

- Create a chase situation with a second defensive end lined up one yard behind the first defensive end. Both defensive ends start on simulated ball snap.
- Set up two drill stations with the loops placed side by side and seven yards apart.
- Set up a figure-eight drill by placing one loop above the other with a two-yard separation between the two loops.
- The drill can be used for all pass-rushing positions.

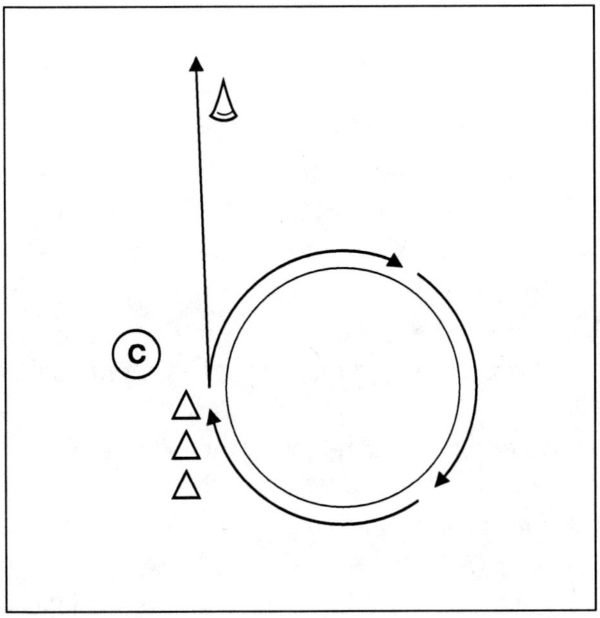

"D" Drill

Jeff Bower
Head Coach, University of Southern Mississippi

Objective: To develop agility and speed. Incorporated are skills related to changing directions.

Equipment Needed: Twenty-two cones

Description:

- Arrange 20 cones to form the capital letter D on a selected yard line. Two additional cones are placed, one five yards to the left of the base of the letter D (cone A) and the other five yards below the left base of the letter D (cone B) (see the diagram).
- Position a defensive end adjacent to the cone that forms the base of the left side of the letter D. The defensive end faces cone A.
- Other defensive ends stand adjacent to the drill area.
- The coach can be positioned either inside or outside of the letter D.
- On the coach's command, the first defensive end drives from his stance and sprints to and around cone A, and then continues his run back to and around the curve of the letter D.
- When the defensive end reaches the top of the left side of the letter D, he runs in and out of the cones that form the left side (straight side) of the letter D.
- The defensive end finishes the drill by sprinting past cone B.
- The drill continues until all defensive ends have had a sufficient number of repetitions, starting from both the top and bottom of the letter D.

Coaching Points:

- Always check to see that the defensive ends are in their proper stances before starting the drill.
- Insist that the drill be conducted at full speed.
- Instruct the defensive end to run the curve with an inside body lean and with the arms pumping.
- Insist that the defensive ends finished the drill by sprinting past cone B.

Safety Considerations:

- Proper warm-up should precede the drill.
- The drill area should be clear of all foreign articles.
- Alert defensive ends who are waiting to perform the drill to stay well clear of the drill-finish area.

Variations:

- The drill can be used as a general speed and agility drill for all positions.
- Substitute a shuffle through the cones that forms the straight line of the letter D.
- When starting the drill, have the defensive ends run and touch cone A instead of running around it.

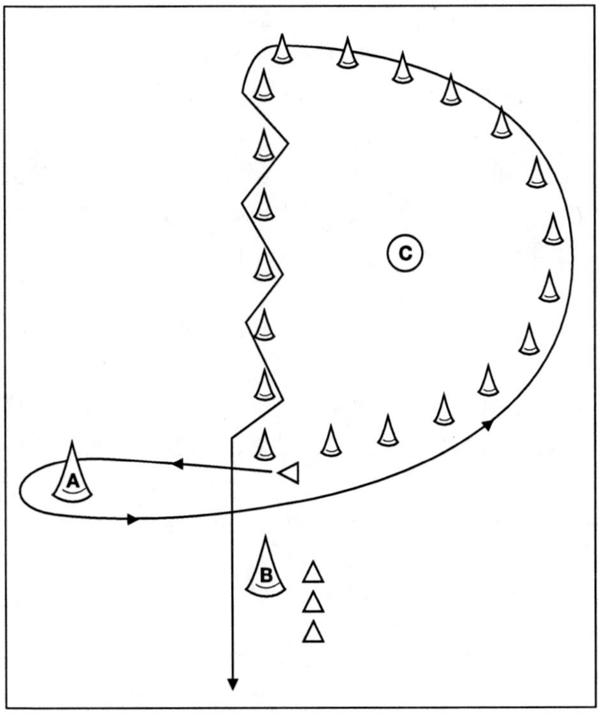

Hoop Cone Competition Drill

Jerry Kill
Head Coach, Southern Illinois University

Objective: To develop agility and speed. Incorporated are skills related to rushing the passer.

Equipment Needed: Two hoops (12 feet each in diameter) and four cones

Description:

- Align two hoops five yards apart on a selected yard line. Place a cone at the inside edge and outside edge of the base of each hoop (see the diagram).
- Position a row of defensive ends next to the outside cone of each hoop.
- The coach stands at the midpoint at the top of and between the two hoops.
- On the coach's command, the first defensive end in each row drives from his three-point stance, races around the hoops, and finishes at the cone at the inside bottom of the hoop.
- The drill continues until all defensive ends have had a sufficient number of repetitions, racing around the hoops from both a left and a right alignment.

Coaching Points:

- Always check to see that the defensive ends are in their proper stances before starting the drill.
- Insist that the drill be conducted at full speed.
- Instruct the defensive ends to lean to the inside, dipping the inside shoulder as they circle the hoops.
- Emphasize the importance of keeping the heads up and arms pumping as the defensive ends circle the hoops.

Safety Considerations:

- Proper warm-up should precede the drill.
- The drill area should be clear of all foreign articles.
- Alert the performing defensive ends to run straight to the finish cone to avoid a possible collision.

Variations:

- The drill can be used for all pass-rushing positions.
- Place the hoops one on top of the other and create a chase situation. Two feet should separate the two hoops. Position one defensive end at the bottom of the top hoop and the other at the base of the bottom hoop.

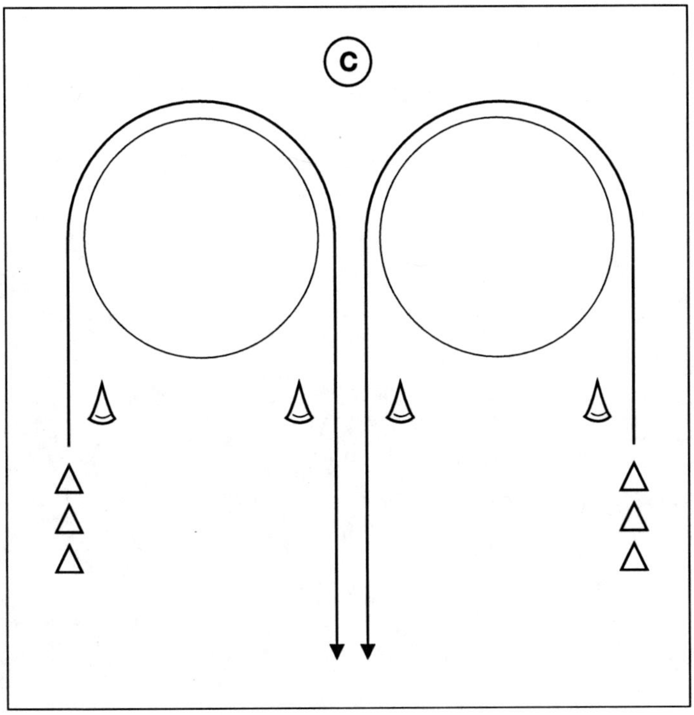

10

General Agility and Speed Drills

Panther Drill

John Fox
Head Coach, Carolina Panthers

Objective: To develop agility and speed. Incorporated are skills related to changing directions.

Equipment Needed: Six cones

Description:

- Place four cones (A, B, C, and D) side by side on the goal line. One yard separates cone A from cone B. Cone C is two yards from cone B, and cone D is two yards from cone C (see the diagram).
- Place two remaining cones (E and F) on the five-yard line. Cone E is placed at the midpoint between cones A and B, and cone F is placed at the midpoint between cones C and D (see the diagram).
- Align the first drill participant on his back behind the goal line and outside of cone A.
- Other drill participants stand adjacent to cone A.
- The coach stands behind cone C.
- On the coach's command, the first drill participant turns to his inside and sprints between cone A and B and then to and around cone E.
- The drill participant sprints back to and around cone C.
- The first drill participant finishes the drill by sprinting to and around cone F and then backpedals back past cone D.
- On the coach's command, the second drill participant starts his run when the first drill participant rounds cone C.
- The drill continues until all drill participants have had a sufficient number of repetitions.
- The drill should be run from both a left and a right alignment.

Coaching Points:

- Always check to see that the drill participants' heads are below the goal line before starting the drill.
- Insist that the drill be conducted at full speed.
- Instruct the drill participants to stay tight to the cones as they run around the cone (no touching the cone should be permitted).
- Insist that the drill participants backpedal at full speed past the goal line.

Safety Considerations:

- Proper warm-up should precede the drill.
- The drill area should be clear of all foreign articles.
- Alert the drill participants who have finished the drill to stay clear of the drill-finish area.

Variations:

- Set up multiple drill stations to create competition between drill participants.
- Put drill participants on a stopwatch to promote competition.

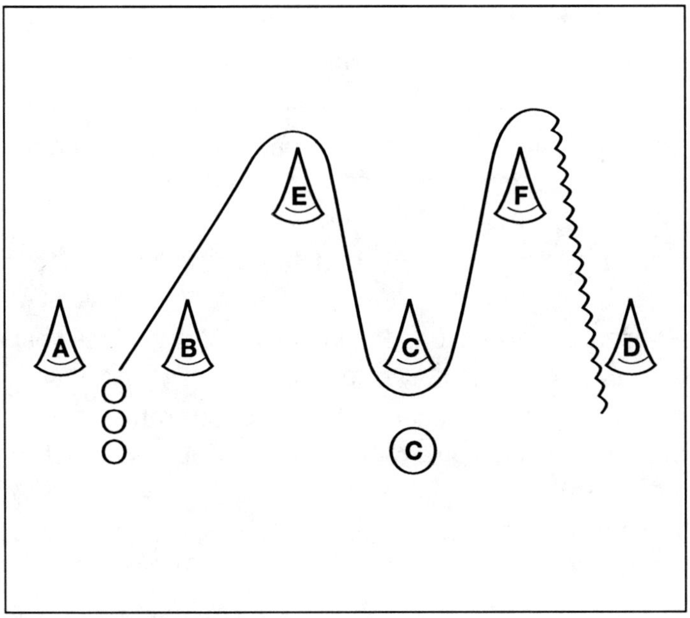

Star Drill

Bobby Johnson
Head Coach, Vanderbilt University

Objective: To develop agility and speed. Incorporated are skills related to changing directions and acceleration.

Equipment Needed: Five cones

Description:

- Place four cones (A, B, C, and D) five yards apart to form a square. A fifth cone is placed in the middle of the square to make a star (see the diagram).
- Align a row of drill participants at the midpoint below cones A and D.
- The coach stands adjacent to the cone, which forms the middle of the star.
- On the coach's command, the first drill participant drives from his stance and touches the middle cone with his right hand. He then turns, sprints back to cone A, and touches cone A with his left hand.
- The drill participant turns and sprints back to the middle cone, touching it with his right hand.
- The drill participant sprints to cone B and touches it with his left hand, and then he sprints back to the middle cone and touches it with his right hand.
- The drill participant sprints to cone C, touching it with his left hand, and then he sprints back to the middle cone with a right-hand touch, and then on to cone D with another left-hand touch.
- The first drill participant finishes the drill by returning for the final time to the middle cone with a right-hand touch, and then he sprints past the midpoint of cones A and D.
- The drill continues until all drill participants have had a sufficient number of repetitions, moving from both a clockwise and counter-clockwise direction. When going in a clockwise direction, the outside cones are touched with the left hand and the middle cone with the right hand; when going in the counter-clockwise direction, the outside cones are touched with the right hand and the middle cone with the left hand.

Coaching Points:

- Always check to see that the drill participants are in their proper stances before starting the drill.
- Insist that the drill be conducted at full speed.

- Instruct the drill participants to keep a low center of gravity and to maintain body control throughout the drill.
- Emphasize the importance of accelerating after each cone is touched.
- Insist that the drill participants finish the drill by sprinting past the midpoint of cones A and D.

Safety Considerations:

- Proper warm-up should precede the drill.
- The drill area should be clear of all foreign articles.
- Alert drill participants who are waiting to perform the drill to stay well clear of the drill-finish area.

Variation:

- Vary the distance between the cones.

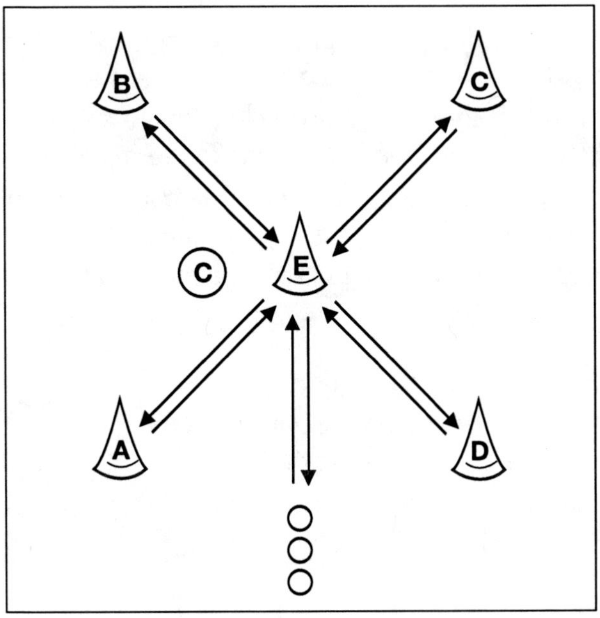

Cone Reaction Drill

Frank Beamer
Head Coach, Virginia Polytechnic Institute

Objective: To develop agility and speed. Incorporated are skills related to reacting and changing directions.

Equipment Needed: Four cones

Description:

- Place four cones seven yards apart to form a square.
- Position a drill participant in the middle of the square (see the diagram).
- Other drill participants stand adjacent to the drill area.
- The coach stands at the midpoint of the base of the square.
- On the coach's command, the first drill participant buzzes his feet in the middle of the square.
- The coach will point to one of the corner cones, and the drill participant will sprint to that cone, touch it, and return to the middle of the square with his feet buzzing.
- The drill continues with the coach pointing to different cones as the drill participant sprints to and touches that cone and returns to the middle cone.
- The first drill participant finishes the drill at the coach's direction by sprinting past the coach.
- The drill continues until all drill participants have had a sufficient number of repetitions.

Coaching Points:

- Always make sure that the drill participants are buzzing their feet and are in a good football ready position before starting the drill.
- Insist that the drill be conducted at full speed.
- Instruct the drill participants to maintain the proper body alignment throughout the drill.
- Insist that the drill participants touch each cone that they are directed to touch.
- The time that each drill participant is performing the drill should be limited to 10 seconds.
- Insist that the drill participants finish the drill by sprinting past the coach.

Safety Considerations:

- Proper warm-up should precede the drill.
- The drill area should be clear all foreign articles

Variations:

- Vary the distances between the cones.
- The drill can use various movements to the cones, including shuffling and carioca.

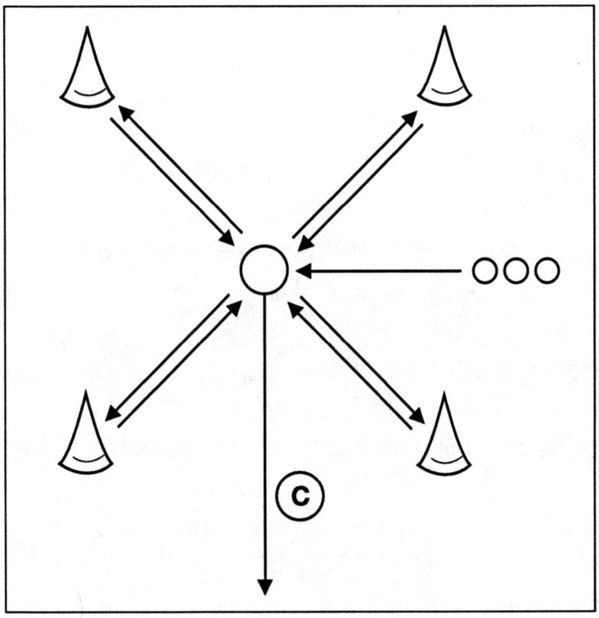

Lateral and Explode Drill

Mike Ledford
Head Coach, University of West Georgia

Objective: To develop agility and speed. Incorporated are skills related to changing directions.

Equipment Needed: Four agility bags and two cones

Description:

- Place four agility bags end-to-end in a vertical plane to a selected yard line. The two middle bags are aligned on the outside edges of the first and last bags. One-and-a-half yards separate the ends of each bag. A cone is placed five yards from and just to the left of the first and last bags (see the diagram).
- Align a row of drill participants adjacent to one of the end cones.
- The coach is positioned on the outside of the second bag.
- On the coach's command, the first drill participant drives from his stance and sprints past the first bag.
- The drill participant works laterally between the first and second bags and then sprints past the second and third bags.
- In finishing the drill, the drill participant works laterally between the third and fourth bags and then sprints past the cone on that end.
- On the coach's command, the second drill participant will start the drill when the first drill participant has worked laterally between the first and second bags.
- The drill continues until all drill participants have had a sufficient number of repetitions, starting from both ends of the bags.

Coaching Points:

- Always check to see that the drill participants are in the appropriate stances before starting the drill.
- Insist that the drill be conducted at full speed.
- Instruct the drill participants to plant the outside foot, glide between the bags, and accelerate past the next two bags.
- Emphasize the importance of keeping a tight relationship to the bags.
- Insist that the drill participants finish the drill by sprinting past the end cone.

Safety Considerations:

- Proper warm-up should precede the drill.
- The drill area should be clear of all foreign articles.
- This drill is not recommended for players with ankle or knee injuries.

Variations:

- Vary the distance between the bags and the cones.
- Vary the distance between the second and third bags.

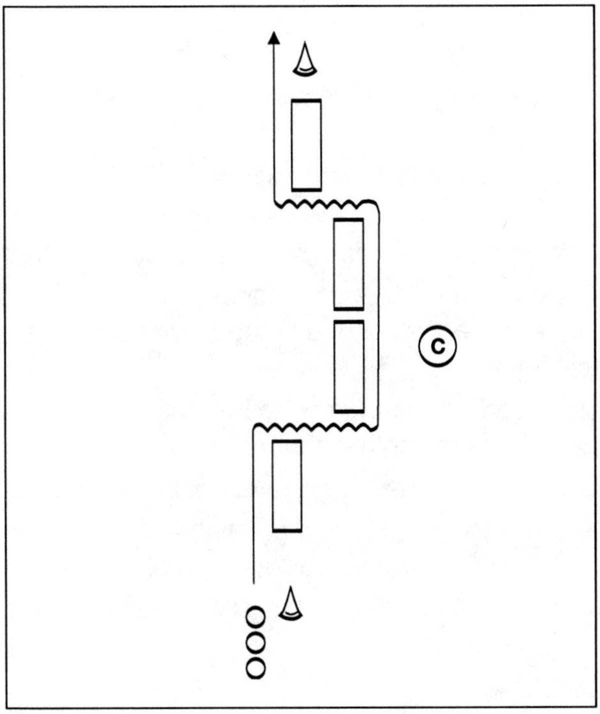

Phoenix Star Drill

Pete Lembo
Head Coach, Elon University

Objective: To develop agility and speed. Incorporated are skills related to changing directions.

Equipment Needed: Eight cones

Description:

- Set up two drill stations by placing four cones eight yards apart to form two squares. Two yards separate each eight-foot square (see the diagram).
- Align a row of drill participants adjacent to the outside cone that forms the base of each square.
- The coach stands at the midpoint and three yards below the two squares.
- On the coach's command, the first drill participant in each row sprints to the center of the square and assumes the football ready position and fires their feet.
- The coach, using both hands to signal, points to a cone in each square, and the two drill participants sprint to and touch the designated cone and then return to the center of the square.
- Once the drill participants have returned to the middle of the square, the coach will immediately signal them to another cone.
- The previous three descriptions are repeated six or seven times.
- On the coach's command ("Out") and pointing his hands over his head, the drill participants sprint out of the square past the coach.
- The drill continues until all participants have had a sufficient number of repetitions.

Coaching Points:

- Always check to see that the drill participants are in the football ready position and firing their feet before starting the drill.
- Insist that the drill be conducted at full speed.
- Instruct the drill participants to maintain the proper body alignment with their heads up and their eyes focused on the coach throughout the drill.
- Emphasize the importance of sprinting to and from the designated cone. Do not allow drill participants to backpedal or shuffle.
- Insist that drill participants finish the drill by sprinting past the coach.

Safety Considerations:

- Proper warm-up should precede the drill.
- The drill area should be clear of all foreign articles.

Variation:

- Vary the distances between the cones.

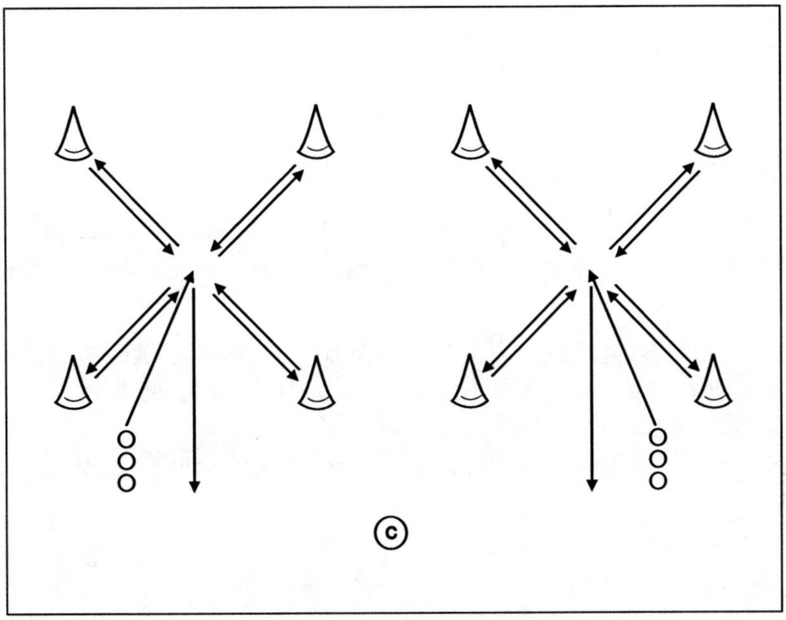

Change of Direction Drill

David Bailiff
Head Coach, Rice University

Objective: To develop agility and speed. Incorporated are skills related to changing directions.

Equipment Needed: None

Description:

- Align two drill participants three yards apart behind a selected yard line (see the diagram).
- Other drill participants stand adjacent to the drill area.
- The coach is positioned five yards in front of and the facing the two drill participants.
- On the coach's command, the first two drill participants assume the football ready position.
- On the coach's hand signals, the drill participants shuffle laterally back and forth.
- After several changes of directions, the drill participants are directed to finish the drill by sprinting past the coach.
- The drill continues until all drill participants have had a sufficient number of repetitions.

Coaching Points:

- Always check to see that the drill participants are in the football ready position before starting the drill.
- Instruct the drill participants as to the proper execution of the shuffle.
- Emphasize the importance of planting the outside foot in making all directional changes.
- Instruct the drill participants to maintain the proper body alignment with the head up and eyes focused on the coach throughout the drill.
- Insist that the drill participants finish the drill by sprinting full speed past the coach.

Safety Considerations:

- Proper warm-up should precede the drill.
- The drill area should be clear of all foreign articles.

Variations:

- Incorporate other movements, such as the carioca, turn-and-sprint, and the backpedal.
- Set up multiple drill stations.

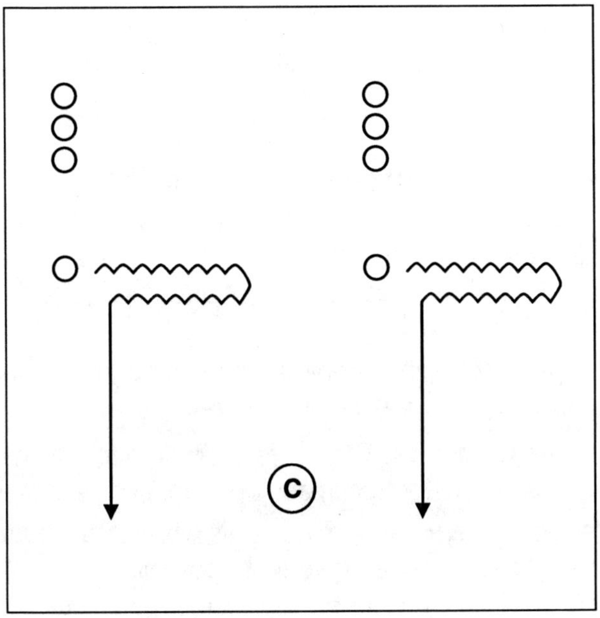

Mirror Shuffle Drill

Andy Talley
Head Coach, Villanova University

Objective: To develop agility and speed. Incorporated are skills related to reacting and changing directions.

Equipment Needed: Two cones and a whistle

Description:

- Place two cones 10 yards apart on a selected yard line.
- Align two drill participants at the midpoint of the two cones. Designate one drill participant the leader and the other the follower. The leader stands on the yard line between the cones, and the follower is positioned five yards from and facing the leader (see the diagram).
- Other drill participants form lines behind the leader and the follower.
- The coach is positioned adjacent to the drill area.
- On the coach's command, ("Set"), the follower moves four yards forward, and both drill participant assume the football ready position, firing their feet.
- On the coach's second command, blowing his whistle, the leader will shuffle back and forth between the cones as quickly as possible as the follower mirrors his every move and maintains a nose-to-nose relationship to the leader.
- The drill continues for five to seven seconds, and on the coach's second whistle, both drill participants turn and sprint past the cone on their right.
- The drill continues until all drill participants have had a sufficient number of repetitions, as both a leader and a follower.

Coaching Points:

- Always check to see that the drill participants are in the football ready position and firing their feet before starting the drill.
- Insist that the drill be conducted at full speed.
- Instruct the drill participants as to the proper execution of the shuffle.
- Emphasize the importance for the follower to maintain the proper mirror alignment to the leader.
- Insist that the drill participants finish the drill by sprinting past the cone on their right side.

Safety Considerations:

- Proper warm-up should precede the drill.
- The drill area should be clear of all foreign articles.

Variations:

- Vary the distance between the two cones.
- The drill can be used as a tackling drill by designating the leader as a ballcarrier and the follower as a defensive player. Finish the drill with the defensive player executing a form tackle on the ballcarrier.

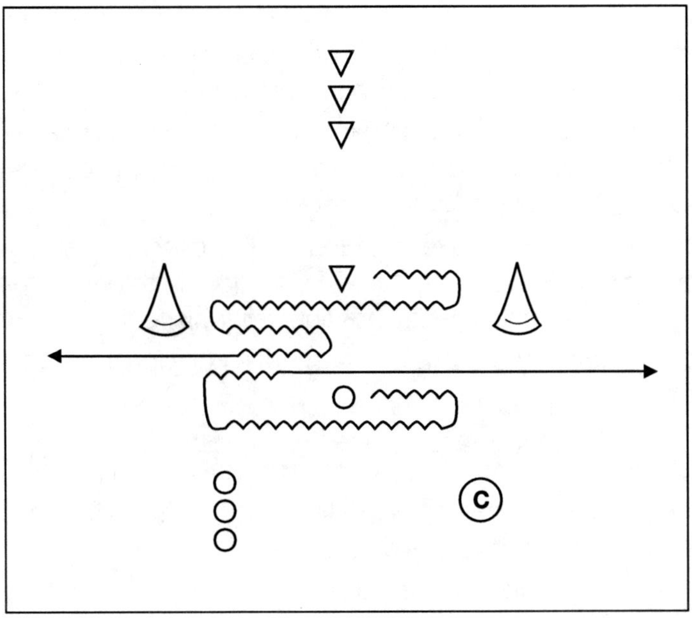

Box Drill

James Reid
Head Coach, Virginia Military Institute

Objective: To develop agility and speed. Incorporated are skills related to changing directions.

Equipment Needed: Four cones

Description:

- Place four cones 10 yards apart to form a box.
- Position a row of drill participants five yards outside and to the right side of the box.
- The coach stands at the midpoint and five yards below the base of the box.
- On the coach's command, the first drill participant sprints to the middle of the box, faces the coach, and assumes the football ready position, firing his feet.
- On the coach's hand signal, pointing to a cone, the first drill participant sprints to that cone. As the drill participant approaches that cone, the coach will redirect the drill participant by pointing to another cone.
- After the drill participant has executed four or five directional changes, and on the coach's command ("Ready, ready"), the drill participant returns to the middle of the box and assume the football ready position, firing his feet.
- On the coach's command ("Fire out"), the drill participant sprints out of the box and past the coach.

Coaching Points:

- Always check to see that the drill participants are in the football ready position and firing their feet before starting the drill.
- Insist that the drill be conducted a full speed.
- Insist that all drill participants finish the drill by sprinting from the middle of the box past the coach.

Safety Considerations:

- Proper warm-up should precede the drill.
- The drill area should be clear of all foreign articles.

Variations:

- Vary the distances between the cones.
- Incorporate different movement patterns, such as the backpedal, the shuffle, and the crossover. The backpedal is used when moving straight back from a front cone to a back cone. The shuffle is used when moving form a side cone to another side cone. The crossover is used when moving diagonally from one corner cone to another corner cone.

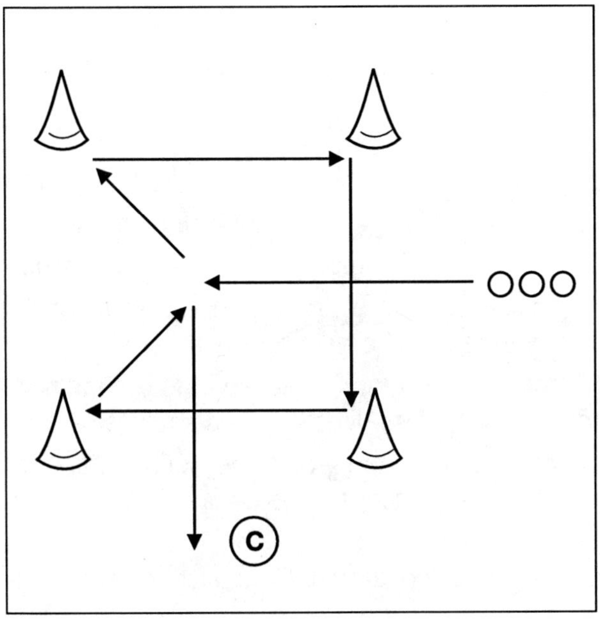

Lateral Out Back Drill

Chuck Lliteras
Assistant Coach, William Jewell College

Objective: To develop agility and speed. Incorporated are skills related to changing directions.

Equipment Needed: Five agility bags

Description:

- Place five agility bags three yards apart and perpendicular to a selected yard line (see the diagram).
- Position a row of drill participants three yards outside and in a sideways alignment to the first bag.
- The coach stands in a front-facing alignment to the first drill participant.
- On the coach's command, the first drill participant assumes the football ready position.
- On the coach's second command, the first drill participant shuffles over the first two bags, placing both feet in the hole between the second and third bags.
- After the second foot hits the ground between the second and third bags, the drill participant immediately changes directions and shuffles back over the second bag.
- Again after the second foot hits the ground between the first and second bags, the drill participant immediately changes directions and shuffles over the second and third bags.
- The previous description is repeated until the first drill participant has shuffled over all five bags.
- When finishing the drill, the drill participant sprints five yards past the last bag.
- The drill continues until all drill participants have had a sufficient number of repetitions, from both a left and a right alignment.

Coaching Points:

- Always check to see that the drill participants assume the football ready position before starting the drill.
- Insist that the drill be conducted at full speed.
- Instruct the drill participants as to the proper execution of the shuffle.
- Emphasize the importance of maintaining the proper body alignment throughout the drill.
- Insist that the drill participant finish the drill by sprinting five yards past the last bag.

Safety Considerations:

- Proper warm-up should precede the drill.
- The drill area should be clear of all foreign articles.

Variations:

- Set up multiple drill stations.
- Have drill participants sprint left or right for five yards after shuffling over the last bag.
- Incorporate a fumble and fumble-recovery situation at the end of the drill instead of the sprint.

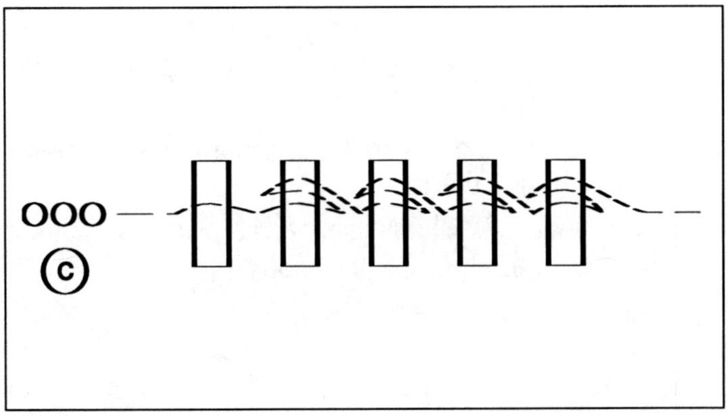

Hounds and Hares Drill

Henry Trevathan
Part-time Coach, Bridgewater College

Objective: To develop speed and agility. Incorporated are skills related to the promotion of camaraderie.

Equipment Needed: A dense wooded area

Description:

- Design and clear a 50-yard obstacle path through a dense wooded area. The path should have many cuts, bends, and logs to run around and jump over.
- Position two drill participants, one five yards behind the other, at the starting point of the obstacle path. Designate the first drill participant as the rabbit and the second as the hound.
- On the coach's command, the two drill participants sprint through the obstacle path with the hound chasing the rabbit.
- The drill continues until all drill participants have had a sufficient number of repetitions, both as the hound and as the rabbit.

Coaching Points:

- Encourage whooping and hollering throughout the drill, as it will build camaraderie and spirit
- Coaches are encouraged to participate in the drill.
- The drill makes for an excellent off-season fun-day activity.

Safety Considerations:

- Proper warm-up should precede the drill.
- The obstacle path should be checked carefully to remove any hazardous objects.

Variation:

- Lengthen the obstacle path and have different positions (quarterbacks and linebackers, etc.) race through the course.

11

Warm-Up Drills

At 45 Drill

Fisher DeBerry
Former Head Coach, United States Air Force Academy

Objective: To allow for the proper warm-up. Incorporated are skill related to changing directions.

Equipment Needed: None

Description:

- Align a row of drill participants on a selected yard line. Five yards separate each drill participant (see the diagram)
- Other drill participants stand adjacent to the drill area.
- The coach stands five yards in front of the first-row drill participants.
- On the coach's command, the drill participants assume the football ready position.
- On the coach's hand signal, pointing either left or right, the drill participants pivot and run back at warm-up speed at a 45-degree angle.
- After the previous description is repeated four or five times, the drill participants finish the drill by turning and jogging past the coach.
- The drill continues until all drill participants have had a sufficient number of repetitions.

Coaching Points:

- Always check to see that the drill participants are in their football ready position before starting the drill.
- Emphasize the importance of maintaining the proper body alignment throughout the drill.

Safety Considerations:

- Proper stretching should precede the drill.
- The drill should progress from warm-up speed to full speed.
- The drill area should be clear of all foreign articles.
- Alert drill participants who are waiting to perform the drill to stay clear of the drill-finish area.

Variation:

- Execute the drill at full speed, and use as a speed and agility drill for all positions.

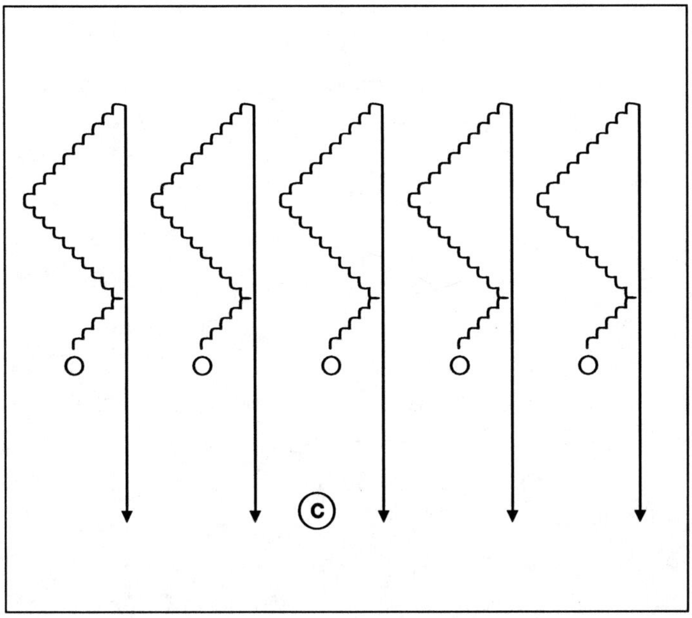
C

All-Purpose Running Drill

Pete Rodriguez
Former Assistant Coach, Jacksonville Jaguars

Objective: To allow for the proper warm-up. Incorporated are skills related to different movement patterns.

Equipment Needed: Twenty-five cones and a whistle

Description:

- Align all drill participants on the goal line, in rows and by position.
- Place cones along the 25-yard line on each sideline, on each hash mark, and at midfield. This cone alignment is repeated on the 50-yard line, the far-side 25-yard line, and on the far-side goal line.
- The coach stands at midfield on the 50-yard line, facing the drill participants.
- On the coach's whistle, the first drill participant in each row assumes the football ready position, jogs to the 25-yard line, strides to the 50-yard line, backpedals to the far 25-yard line, and cariocas past the far goal line.
- When the first drill participant in each row reaches the 25-yard line, the coach blows the whistle for the second drill participant in each row to begin his movement down the field.
- The drill continues until all drill participants have had a sufficient number of repetitions of each movement pattern, moving back and forth and up and down the football field, from goal line to goal line.

Coaching Points:

- Check to see that all drill participants are in the football ready position before starting the drill.
- Instruct the drill participants to the proper execution of all movement patterns.
- Emphasize the importance of executing the different movement patterns correctly.

Safety Considerations:

- Proper stretching should precede the drill.
- The drill area (especially the sideline areas) should be clear of all foreign articles.

Variation:

- Change the sequence of the various movement patterns in moving up and down the football field.

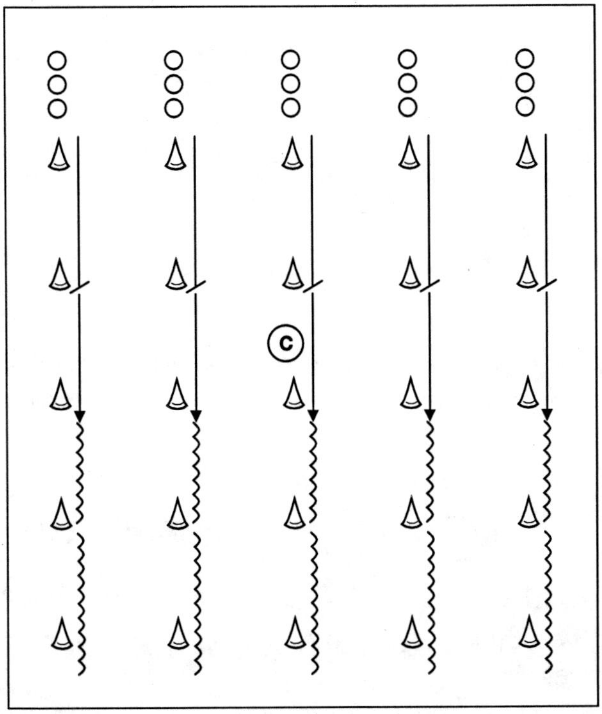
C

Active/Dynamic Warm-Up Drill

Jimmye Laycock
The College of William and Mary

Objective: To allow for proper warm-up through various stretching movements.

Equipment Needed: A whistle

Description:

- Align the drill participants in exercise rows across the football field. Five yards separate each row of drill participants and five yards separate the drill participants in each row.
- The coach stands in front of the drill area.
- On the coach's whistle, the drill participants execute one of the following stretching movements:
  - ✓ Knee to chest—One knee is pulled up to the chest, and at the same time the toes should be pushing up on the opposite foot. The movement is repeated with both knees.
  - ✓ Hamstring kick—One leg is kicked up and touches the opposite arm, which is extended out at a right angle. The movement is repeated with both legs.
  - ✓ Lunge and twist—One leg is extended forward while the opposite knee is dropped to the ground. The upper torso is twisted toward the extended leg. The movement is repeated with both legs.
  - ✓ Lateral lunge—One leg is extended to the side, and the body is leaned in that direction, which in turn straightens the opposite leg. The movement is repeated with both legs.
  - ✓ Quad stretch—One foot is pulled up to the butt while the toes on the opposite foot are extended. The movement is repeated with both feet.
  - ✓ High knee—Each knee is brought up to the chest, as in a running motion, with arms pumping. The movement is repeated with both knees.
  - ✓ Butt kick—Each foot is kicked back, trying to hit the butt with the heel. The movement is repeated with both feet.
- The drill continues until all drill participants have had a sufficient number of repetitions of each stretching movement.

Coaching Point:

- Instruct the drill participants as to the proper execution of each of the stretching movements.

Safety Consideration:

- The drill area should be clear of all foreign articles.

Variation:

- Incorporate other stretching movements.

Team Dynamic Warm-Up Drill

Jack Siedlecki
Head Coach, Yale University

Objective: To allow for proper warm-up. Incorporated are skills related to different movement patterns.

Equipment Needed: A whistle

Description:

- Align rows of drill participants on opposite sidelines and on alternating five-yard lines, facing the field.
- The coach, with a whistle, is positioned in the middle of the football field.
- On the coach's whistle, the first drill participant in each row and on both sides of the field moves across the field in one of the following movement patterns:
  - ✓ High knee grab (five strides), lunge with reach (five strides), jog to the far sideline
  - ✓ Butt kick to the near hash, high knees to the far hash, power skip to the far sideline
  - ✓ Five strides of speed bounding to build up to a run at 75-percent speed to the far hash, jog to the far sideline
  - ✓ Lateral lunge right (five strides), carioca right (five strides), shuffle right (five strides), jog to the far sideline
  - ✓ Lateral lunge left (five strides), carioca left (five strides), shuffle left (five strides), jog to the far sideline
- After the first row of drill participants on each sideline has advanced 10 yards, the coach blows the whistle to begin moving the second row of drill participants across the field.
- The drill continues until all drill participants have had a sufficient number of repetitions of all movement patterns.
- To finish the drill, the coach blows the whistle three times, and all drill participants come together for a breakdown.

Coaching Points:

- Instruct the drill participants as to the proper execution of all movement patterns.
- Emphasize the importance of executing the different movement patterns correctly.

Safety Considerations:

- Proper stretching should precede the drill.
- The drill area (especially the sideline areas) should be clear of all foreign articles.

Variation:

- Incorporate other movement patterns.

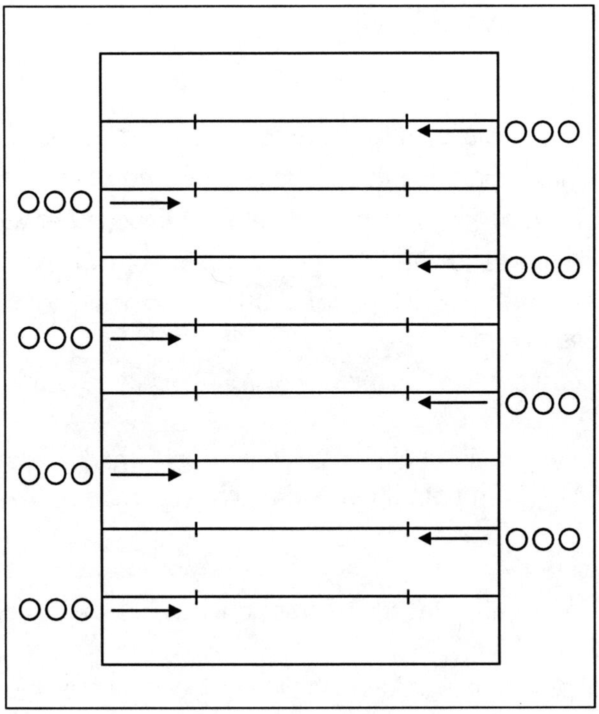

Box Warm-Up Drill

Mickey Brown *(deceased)*
Former Assistant Coach, Duke University
(Drill submitted by Glen Ellis)

Objective: To allow for the proper warm-up. Incorporated are skills related to changing directions.

Equipment Needed: Four cones

Description:

- Align four cones (A, B, C, and D) seven yards apart to form a square (see the diagram).
- Position a row of drill participants behind and outside of cone A.
- The coach stands three yards behind and at the midpoint between cones A and D.
- On the coach's command, the first drill participant jogs to cone B.
- After rounding cone B, the drill participant jogs diagonally to and rounds cone D, and then he jogs to cone C.
- The first drill participant finishes the drill by rounding cone C, and jogging diagonally past cone A.
- The drill continues until all drill participants have had a sufficient number of repetitions, starting from both a left and a right alignment.

Coaching Points:

- Always check to see that the drill participants are in their proper stance before starting the drill.
- Instruct the drill participants to lower their center of gravity as they round the cones.
- Emphasize the importance of keeping the head and eyes focused ahead.

Safety Considerations:

- Proper stretching should precede the drill.
- The drill area should be clear of all foreign articles.
- Alert the drill participants who are waiting to perform the drill to stay clear of the drill-finish area.

Variations:

- The drill can be used as a speed and agility drill for all positions.
- Vary the distances between the cones.
- Set up multiple drill stations.

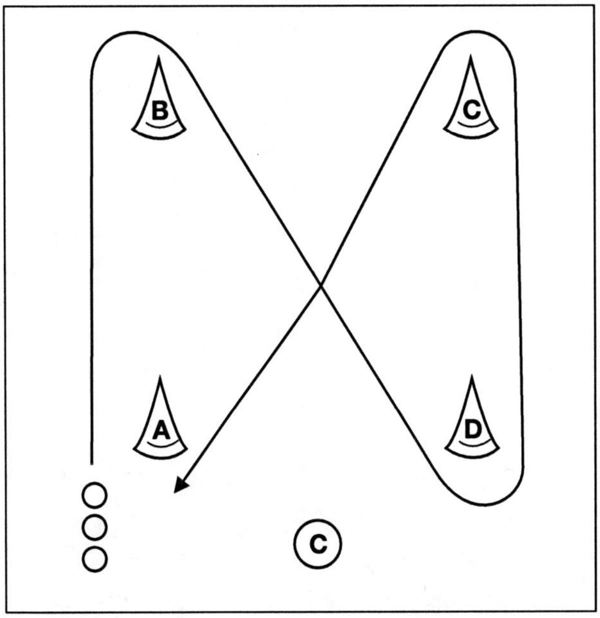
B
C
A
D
C

Cowboy Warm-Up Drill

Joe Glenn
Head Coach, University of Wyoming

Objective: To allow for the proper warm-up. Incorporated are skills related to various movement pattern.

Equipment Needed: Whistle

Description:

- Align all drill participants in rows, and by positions, on a selected yard line. Three yards separate each row.
- A coach is positioned at the midpoint and five yards in front of the drill participants.
- On the coach's whistle, the first drill participant in each row drives out of his stance at half speed and runs past the coach.
- The drill continues until all drill participants have had a sufficient number of repetitions of driving out of their stances and running at half speed past the coach.

Coaching Points:

- Check to see that all drill participants are in their proper stances before starting the drill.
- Instruct the drill participants to keep their heads up and their eyes focused straight ahead.
- Emphasize the importance of maintaining the proper body alignment throughout the drill.

Safety Considerations:

- Proper stretching should precede the drill.
- The drill area should be clear of all foreign articles.

Variations:

- Have the drill participants run at half speed for various distances, such as 10 yards, 15 yards, etc.
- Have the drill participants run at three-quarter speed.
- Have the drill participants execute other movement patterns, such as the backpedal, shuffle, or carioca. In executing the shuffle and carioca, the drill participants should turn and face the same sideline.

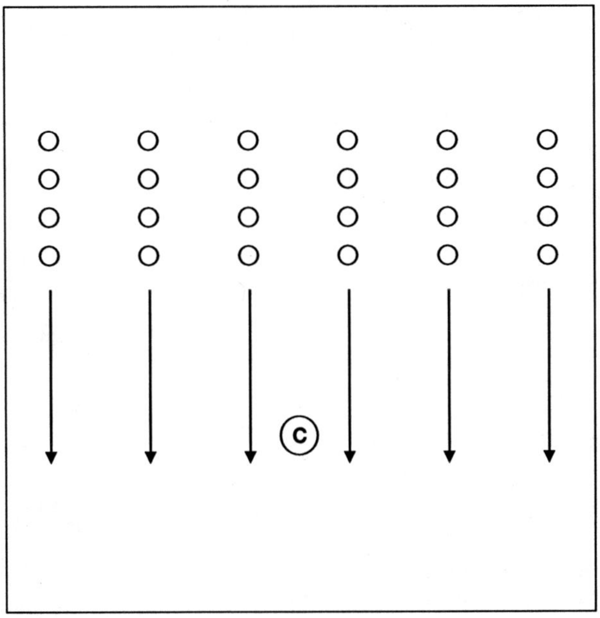
C

Dynamic Warm-Up Drill

Jon Heacock
Head Coach, Youngstown State University

Objective: To allow for a proper warm-up. Incorporated are skills related to the execution of various movement patterns.

Equipment Needed: Whistle

Description:

- Align all drill participants across the football field by position or class.
- The coach is positioned in front of and facing the drill participants.
- On the coach's command, the drill participants execute the various movement patterns that follow:
  - ✓ Walking lunges—The athlete lifts the right leg to waist level and steps forward onto a flexed knee, making sure the toes are positioned in front of the knee. The left leg should flex with the movement so that the left knee stops just above the ground. The athlete transitions into the next step, with the left leg following the same pattern. He should maintain an erect posture throughout the pattern. Arm action should imitate a running motion. The athlete performs the walking lunge for 15 yards, and then jogs the remaining 15 yards. Repeat two times.
  - ✓ Shuffle squats—The athlete side-steps into an athletic stance (i.e., the feet are hip-width apart), and then immediately lowers to a full-body squat. At the bottom of the squat position, he presses outward on the knees with the hands and elbows to actively stretch the groin. He must keep an erect posture with the feet flat during the entire drill. From the bottom position, he hops or shuffles into another squat. He performs a shuffle squat for 15 yards, and then jogs the remaining 15 yards. Repeat two times.
  - ✓ Walking toe touches—The athlete kicks forward with the right leg (maintaining a straight-leg position) to at least waist level and reaches with the opposite hand to touch the right toes. During the kick, the left leg should also remain straight. The athlete immediately alternates the same movement to the left leg. He must keep an erect posture through the entire series of toe touches. He walks and kicks for 15 yards, and then jogs the remaining 15 yards. Repeat two times.
  - ✓ High-step cariocas—The athlete performs this step in the same manner as the traditional carioca (leads with the right leg, steps behind with the left leg, leads with the right leg, steps in front with the left leg). In this variation, the athlete exaggerates the front step by driving the knee up to waist level or higher. He cariocas for 15 yards, and then jogs the remaining 15 yards. Repeat two times.

- ✓ Burpees—The athlete performs this drill standing in one spot. From the standing position, he performs a full-body squat so that the hands can be placed flat on the ground just beside the ankles. From this position, he thrusts the legs out behind the body so that he lands in a push-up position. He performs a push-up, jumps back into the full-body squat, and returns to the standing position. He performs 10 repetitions, and then jogs 30 yards. Repeat two times.
- ✓ Inchworm—The athlete begins in a position flexed at the waist and with the fingers touching the toes. The legs should remain straight through the entire drill. From this bent-over position, the athlete walks out on the hands into a push-up position. From the push-up position, he inches the feet forward with small steps until he is again in the bent-over position. He must keep the legs straight during the entire exercise. He performs the inchworm for 15 yards, and then jogs the remaining 15 yards. Repeat two times.
- ✓ High-knees run—The athlete must focus on bringing the knees to at least waist level in short steps. Arm and leg action should be rapid, and the body should be in an erect posture. The athlete performs the high knees for 15 yards, and then jogs the remaining 15 yards. Repeat two times.
- ✓ Light run—The athlete must focus on full striding. He should not reach to achieve a longer stride. He must make sure that the feet contact the ground under the body. He should increase the stride by driving off the ground leg during the strides. The athlete must maintain an erect posture during the exercise. He performs the light run for 30 yards. Repeat two times.
- ✓ Hard run—The athlete performs this drill by combining the high-knees exercise and the light-run exercise. He must focus on technique. He should perform this less-than-full-speed run for 30 yards. Repeat two times.
- ✓ Sprint—The athlete performs a maximal-effort run for 30 yards. Again, he must focus on technique. Repeat two times.

- The drill continues until all drill participants have performed a sufficient number of repetitions of the various movement patterns.

Coaching Points:

- Always check to see that all drill participants are in their designated stances before starting the drill.
- Instruct the drill participant as to the proper execution of the various movement patterns.

Safety Considerations:

- Proper stretching should precede the drill.
- The drill area (especially the sidelines areas) should be clear of all foreign articles.

c

Backpedal-Carioca-Jog Drill

Ron Case
Former Assistant Coach, University of North Carolina

Objective: To allow for proper warm-up. Incorporated are skills related to various movement patterns.

Equipment Needed: None

Description:

- Align rows of drill participants on the sideline facing the field on every five-yard line.
- A coach is positioned at the midpoint and in front of the drill participants at the onside hash mark. A second coach is positioned at the backside hash mark and also faces the drill participants.
- On the front coach's command, the first drill participant in each row assumes the football ready position and backpedals at half speed to the onside hash marks.
- When the drill participants reach the onside hash marks and on the front coach's second command, the drill participants execute a half turn to their left and carioca at half speed to the backside hash marks.
- After the drill participants reach the backside hash marks and on the second coach's command, the drill participants execute a half turn to their left and jog to the far sideline.
- On the front coach's command, the second row of drill participants begin their backpedal at the same time that the first row of drill participants begin their cariocas.
- The drill continues with the drill participants moving back and forth across the field until all drill participants have had a sufficient number of repetitions.

Coaching Points:

- Always check to see that all drill participants are in the football ready position before starting the drill.
- Instruct the drill participants to bend their knees, keeping their hips down and their shoulders straight in front of the knees and with the elbows in tight with the arm pumping in executing the backpedal.
- Instruct the drill participants to keep their hips low and their eyes focused straight ahead in executing the carioca.
- Insist that drill participants finish the drill by jogging past the far sideline.

Safety Considerations:

- The drill area (especially the sideline areas) should be clear of all foreign articles.
- Alert drill participants who have finished the drill to stay clear of the drill-finish area.

Variations:

- Change the sequence of the different move patterns (jog, backpedal, and carioca, or carioca, jog, and backpedal).
- The drill can be used as a general speed and agility drill for all positions.
- The drill can be used as a team-conditioning drill.
- Have drill participants perform the various movement patterns at full speed and for a longer duration.

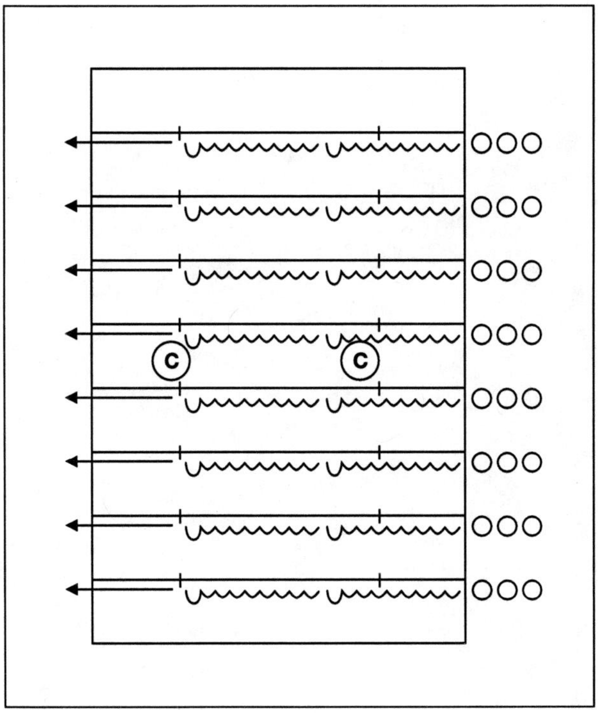

Appendices

Appendix A

Sports Medicine Guidelines*

Dr. Fred Mueller
University of North Carolina-Chapel Hill

Dr. Fred Mueller is Professor and Chairman of the Department of Exercise and Sport Science at The University of North Carolina at Chapel Hill. He currently serves as Director of the National Center for Catastrophic Sports Injury Research at UNC and is Chairman of the American Football Coaches Association Committee on Football Injuries. He is also a member of the American College of Sports Medicine. The following are his recommendations to help reduce football injuries and make the game safer for the participants.

Medical Exam

Mandatory medical examinations and medical history should be taken before allowing an athlete to participate in football. The National Collegiate Athletic Association recommends a thorough medical examination when the athlete first enters the college athletic program and an annual health-history update with use of referral exams when warranted. If the physician or coach has any questions about the athletes' readiness to participate, the athlete should not be allowed to play. High school coaches should follow the recommendations set by their state high school athletic association.

Health Insurance

Each student athlete should be covered by individual, parental, or institutional medical insurance to defray the costs of significant injury or illness. At the high school level, the schools should provide information about association-provided medical insurance.

Preseason Conditioning

All personnel concerned with training football athletes should emphasize proper, gradual, and complete physical conditioning. Special emphasis should be placed on working in hot and humid weather conditions. Recommendations are as follows:

- Athletes must have a physical examination with a history of previous heat illness and type of training activities before organized practice begins.

- Acclimate athletes to heat gradually by providing graduated practice sessions for the first 7 to 10 days and other abnormally hot or humid days.
- Know both the temperature and humidity since it is more difficult for the body to cool itself in high humidity. The use of a sling psychrometer is recommended to measure the relative humidity and anytime the wet-bulb temperature is over 78 degrees practice should be altered.
- Adjust activity levels and provide frequent rest periods. Rest in cool, shaded areas with some air movement and remove helmets and loosen or remove jerseys. Rest periods of 15 to 30 minutes should be provided during workouts of one hour.
- Provide adequate cold water replacement during practice. *Water should always be available and in unlimited quantities to the athletes—give water regularly.*
- Salt should be replaced daily and a liberal salting of the athletes' food will accomplish this purpose. Coaches should not give salt tablets to athletes. Attention must be given to water replacement.
- Athletes should weigh each day before and after practice. Weight charts should be checked each day in order to treat athletes who lose excessive weight.
- Clothing is important and a player should avoid using long sleeves and any excess clothing. Never use rubberized clothing or sweat suits.
- Some athletes are more susceptible to heat injury than others. These individuals are not accustomed to working out in the heat, may be overweight, or may be the eager athlete who constantly competes at his capacity. Athletes with previous heat problems should be watched closely.
- It is important to observe for signs of heat illness. Some trouble signs are nausea, incoherence, fatigue, weakness, vomiting, weak rapid pulse, flushed appearance, visual disturbance, and unsteadiness. If heat illness is suspected, seek a physician's immediate service.

Facilities

It is the responsibility of the school administration to provide excellent facilities for the athletic program. The coach must monitor these facilities and keep them in the best condition.

Emergency Procedures

Each institution should strive to have a certified athletic trainer who is also a member of the school faculty. A team physician should be available for all games and readily available in other situations. There should also be a written emergency-procedure plan in place for catastrophic or serious injuries. All of the trainers and coaches should be familiar with the emergency plan.

Head and Neck Injuries

Coaches should continue to teach and emphasize the proper fundamentals of blocking and tackling to help reduce head and neck injuries. When a player has experienced or shown signs of head trauma (loss of consciousness, visual disturbances, headache, inability to walk correctly, obvious disorientation, memory loss), he should receive immediate medical attention and should not be allowed to return to practice or a game without permission from the proper medical authorities.

Records

Adequate and complete records of each injury should be kept and analyzed to determine injury patterns and to make recommendations for prevention.

Final Recommendations

- Strict enforcement of the rules of the game by both coaches and officials will help reduce injuries.
- You must keep the head out of blocking and tackling. *Keep the head out of football.*
- There should be a renewed emphasis on employing well-trained athletic personnel, providing excellent facilities, and securing the safest and best equipment available.

* Reprinted with permission from *101 Winning Football Drills: From the Legends of the Game* by Jerry Tolley

Appendix B

Medical and Legal Considerations*

Dr. Herb Appenzeller
Guilford College

Dr. Herb Appenzeller is a former athletics director at Guilford College and Professor of Sports Management Emeritus. He is also a former football coach. He has authored and edited 16 books in the area of sport law, risk management, and sport management. He is the co-editor of *From The Gym To The Jury*, a sport-law newsletter. He is a member of four sports Halls of Fame. At the present, he is Executive-in-Residence in graduate Sport Administration at Appalachian State University.

No one wants an athlete to be injured. In sports activities, however, there is always the possibility of injury no matter how careful you are in observing proper procedures. And no one wants to be involved in a lawsuit. Today we have an unprecedented number of sports-related litigation that concerns everyone associated with sports.

The fact that injury occurs does not necessarily mean that the coach is negligent or liable for damages. No sure criteria exist for determining what is negligent action since each case stands individually on its own merit. The following recommendations can help prevent situations that may lead to injuries or litigation:

- Require a thorough physical examination before the athlete engages in the sport.
- Assign someone to make certain all equipment fits properly.
- Assign someone to inspect equipment for defects and the facilities for hazards. Keep an accurate record of each inspection.
- Obtain medical insurance coverage for the athlete and liability insurance for the coaches and other staff members.
- Adopt a medical plan for emergency treatment for all athletes involved in physical contact or strenuous exercise.
- Assign drills within the athlete's range of ability and commensurate with his size, skill, and physical condition.
- Prepare the athlete gradually for all physical drills and progress from simple to complex tasks in strenuous and dangerous drills.

- Warn the athlete of all possible dangers inherent in the drills in which he is involved.
- Follow the activities as designed. If the coach deviates from the prescribed drills, the decision to do so should be based on sound reasoning. Extra precautions for safety should be taken.
- Adopt a policy regarding injuries. Do not attempt to be a medical specialist in judging the physical condition of an athlete under your care.
- Require a physician's medical permission before permitting seriously injured or ill athletes to return to normal practice.
- Avoid moving the injured athlete until it is safe to do so. Whenever the athlete is moved, make certain he is taken away from potentially dangerous playing areas.
- Conduct periodic medical/legal in-service training programs for all personnel.

Risk management has become a vital part of the overall athletics program and football coaches should develop risk management strategies as they relate to their use of drills such as:

- Avoid terminology such as *suicide drills, death run, and hamburger drill.* These terms could come back to haunt you in court.
- In the event of an injury, always follow up with a call or visit to check on the athlete's condition. However, never, never admit fault or assign blame.
- Isolate and keep under lock and key equipment involved in a serious injury (helmet, protective pads, etc.).
- Be aware that you can be sued, but don't panic. Be prepared and coach with confidence.

* Reprinted with permission from *101 Winning Football Drills: From the Legends of the Game* by Jerry Tolley

Appendix C

Summer Two-A-Day Practice Guidelines*

The American Football Coaches Association and the National Athletic Trainers' Association have launched a new educational initiative, HEAT (Helping Educate Athletes in Training). The program is designed to help coaches better prepare their athletes for the grueling conditions of two-a-day practices.

These two-a-day workouts allow for accelerated physical conditioning, increased strength training, and skill development, and can even help develop bonds between teammates. But because these workouts usually occur in hot summer months, heat-related stress becomes a serious concern. Studies have shown that football players can lose dangerously high levels of fluid in 24 hours during two-a-day workouts. Additionally, athletes who are not properly acclimatized to the heat are highly susceptible to injury.

Tips for Safer Two-A-Days

Injury rates increase during two-a-day workouts whether athletes are in peak physical condition or not. In fact, many athletes don't even make their starting lineup because of injuries incurred during preseason training. The following tips can help ensure that athletes stay at their best and prevent heat-related injuries during two-a-days.

Encourage Athletes to Begin Conditioning Before Two-A-Days

Encourage athletes to begin conditioning in the heat two weeks before official practice begins. This allows their bodies to cool more efficiently by increasing sweat production sooner than when they are not acclimated to the heat.

Avoid Workouts During Unusually Hot Temperature

Practice sessions during unusually hot and humid conditions should be limited to very moderate workouts, postponed until cooler time of the day, or brought inside to avoid the heat.

Make Fluids Part of the Playbook

Before, during, and after competition, be sure to consume adequate amounts of fluid. Athletes can make sure they are properly hydrated by checking their urine color: lighter

Printed with the permission of the **AFCA and the **NATA** from their summer **HEAT** publication.*

urine color indicates athletes are better hydrated. The longer the workout session, the more frequently fluids need to be replaced. Research shows that a sports drink containing a six percent carbohydrate solution, like Gatorade, can be absorbed as rapidly as water. But unlike water, a sports drink can provide energy, delay fatigue, and improve performance.

Use the Shade

Before practice, warm up in the shade and be sure to rest in the shade during breaks. Even during rest, exposure to heat can raise the body temperature, increase fluid loss, and decrease the blood available to the muscles during workouts.

Recommend Wearing Loose Fitting Clothing

Cotton blend, loose fitting clothing can help promote heat loss. The rule: the less clothing, the better.

Be Prepared for an Emergency

Always have a cell phone on hand and be familiar with emergency numbers. Also keep ice and ice towels on hand in case of heat-related emergencies.

Fluids Guidelines for Two-A-Days

Proper hydration is the best safeguard against heat illness. Remember to have athletes drink before, during, and after training and competition. The following fluid consumption guidelines can help safeguard athletes against heat-related illness.

Before Exercise

- Two to three hours before exercise drink at least 17 to 20 oz. of water or sports drink.
- Ten to twenty minutes before exercise drink another 7 to 10 oz. of water or sports drink.

What to Drink During Exercise

- Drink early—even minimal dehydration compromises performance. In general, every 10 to 20 minutes drink at least 7 to 10 oz. of water or sports drink. To maintain hydration remember to drink beyond thirst. Optimally, drink fluids based on amount of heat and urine loss.
- Athletes benefit in many situations from drinking a sports drink containing carbohydrate.
- If exercise lasts more than 45 to 50 minutes or is intense, a sports drink should be provided during the session.

- The carbohydrate concentration in the ideal fluid replacement solution should be in the range of six to eight percent (14 g/8 oz.).
- During events when a high rate of fluid intake is necessary to sustain hydration, sport drink with less than seven percent carbohydrate should be used to optimize delivery.
- Fluids with salt (sodium chloride) are beneficial to increasing thirst and voluntary fluid intake as well as offsetting the amount in lost sweat.
- Cool beverages at temperatures of 50 to 59 degrees Fahrenheit are recommended.

What Not to Drink During Exercise

- Fruit juices, carbohydrate gels, sodas, and those sports drinks that have carbohydrate levels greater than 8% area not recommended as the sole beverage.
- Beverages containing caffeine, alcohol, and carbonation are discouraged during exercises because they can dehydrate the body by stimulating excess urine production, or decrease voluntary fluid intake.

After Exercises

Immediately after training or competition is the key time to replace fluids. Weigh athletes before and after exercise. Research indicates that for every pound of weight lost, athletes should drink at least 20 oz. of fluid to optimize rehydration. Sports beverages are an excellent choice.

About the Author

Jerry Tolley is the former head football coach at Elon University. Under his leadership, Elon gained a 49-11-2 record, claiming consecutive national titles in 1980 and 1981. His 1977 and 1978 squads were also nationally ranked number six and number two, respectively. During his five-year head-coaching career, his teams garnered an 8-1 record in playoff bowl competition and won an impressive 80.6 percent of all games played.

During his career, Tolley received numerous coaching honors, including conference, district, area, state, and national coach-of-the-year awards. In January 2003, Tolley received the lifetime membership award from the American Football Coaches Association, and in June 2003, he received the Johnny Vaught Lifetime Achievement Award from the All-American Football Foundation. He has also received the National Football Foundation Hall of Fame Dwight D. Eisenhower Award as well as the State of North Carolina Laurel Wreath award, the highest award given by the state of North Carolina in the area of sports and athletics. Tolley is also a member of Omicron Delta Kappa, the national leadership fraternity.

Tolley is listed in numerous *Who's Who* volumes, including Marquis Who's Who in America, in the World, in the South and Southwest, in Education, in Business and Finance, and in Science and Engineering. He is also listed in Who's Who Among Community Leaders in America, Who's Who in Government Services, and Who's Who Among World Intellectuals.

Tolley's first book, *The American Football Coaches Guide Book To Championship Football Drill,* was published in 1984. His second book, *101 Winning Football Drills: From the Legends Of The Game,* was released in 2003. *The Complete Book of Defensive Football Drills* and *The Complete Book of Offensive Football Drills* followed in 2005. He has also written numerous football related articles for *Coach and Athlete, The Athletic Journal, The Coaching Clinic,* and the *Journal of Health Physical Education, Recreation, and Dance.* His doctoral dissertation was "The History of Intercollegiate Athletics for Men at Elon College."

Since his retirement from coaching, Tolley continues to serve Elon University as the director of annual giving and director of The Elon Society. Tolley is also involved in a number of community activities, and he is currently serving his third term as mayor of the Town of Elon, as well as serving on many local boards, including the Alamance Community Foundation (as chairman), the Thomas E. Powell Jr. Biology Foundation, and BeActive North Carolina.